Beginning Dakota / Tokaheya Dakota Iapi Kin

Beginning Dakota /
Tokaheya Dakota Iapi Kin

24 LANGUAGE AND GRAMMAR LESSONS WITH GLOSSARIES

Nicolette Knudson

Jody Snow

Clifford Canku

MINNESOTA HISTORICAL SOCIETY PRESS

Made possible in part by the Arts and Cultural Heritage Fund through the vote of Minnesotans on November 4, 2008. Administered by the Minnesota Historical Society.

Original publication: © 2003 Owasiŋ k̇aiṡ Owasiŋṡŋi Publishing

www.mhspress.org

The Minnesota Historical Society Press is a member of the Association of American University Presses.

Manufactured in the United States of America.

10 9 8 7 6 5 4 3 2 1

♾ The paper used in this publication meets the minimum requirements of the American National Standard for Information Sciences—Permanence for Printed Library Materials, ANSI Z39.48-1984.

International Standard Book Number
ISBN 13: 978-0-87351-780-5 (paper)

Library of Congress Cataloging-in-Publication Data

Knudson, Nicolette.
    Beginning Dakota — Tokaheya Dakota Iapi Kin : 24 language and grammar lessons with glossaries / Nicolette Knudson, Jody Snow, Clifford Canku.
        p.   cm.
    Previous title: Beginning Dakota Language, 2003.
    ISBN 978-0-87351-780-5 (pbk. : alk. paper)
        1. Dakota language—Study and teaching. 2. Dakota language—Grammar. I. Snow, Jody. II. Canku, Clifford. III. Minnesota Historical Society. IV. Title.
PM1021.K68   2010
497'.5243071—dc22
                                                                                2010030624

Contents

Foreword

The work on this book began when we, as Dakota language students at the University of Minnesota, Morris, approached our instructor, Mr. Clifford Canku, about creating some helpful exercises and strategies for teaching the language. Canku, elder of the Sisseton Wahpeton Dakota Oyate and assistant professor of practice at North Dakota State University embraced the idea and has made this project possible by providing ideas and the cultural contributions found in the book. *Beginning Dakota / Tokaheya Dakota Iapi kin* was initially written specifically for his classes and would not exist if not for his guidance, encouragement, and wisdom.

The book is meant to present another tool in teaching the language. There are many different and effective methods of teaching, including the traditional oral teachings of the Dakota. One intention of this workbook is to help those students who learn well with written and visual methods. The ultimate goal of this workbook is to teach the language in a clear and progressive manner, to allow others the honor of learning Dakota, and to preserve it for the next generation. We'd like to stress that the culture of the Dakota people is not captured in this workbook. **Pidauŋyayapi!**

Nicolette J. Knudson, member of the Sisseton Wahpeton Dakota Oyate
Jody L. Snow, author and language instructor

Beginning Dakota / Tokaheya Dakota Iapi Kin

Lesson One:
The Dakota People

The Great Sioux Nation

The main focus of this workbook is on the Sisseton and Wahpeton Dakota and their language. Although we focus mainly on them, they are part of a much larger nation with similar languages and culture. Here we offer a very brief historical overview.

Three major dialects divide the Great Sioux Nation. A dialect is a form of a language that is specific to a region or group and is usually a member of a larger family of languages. These dialects are called Dakota, Lakota, and Nakota, and these three divisions are also referred to as the Santee (Dakota) Division, the Teton (Lakota) Division, and the Yankton (Nakota) Division. Though divided into these linguistic, or language, groups, they still comprise one large national entity. The people who make up these groups also call themselves the Dakota/Lakota/Nakota Nation. Dakota means "friend" or "friendly." The word *Sioux* is not a Dakota word. This name was given to the Dakota by their neighbors, the Ojibwe (Algonquian). When the French asked the Ojibwe who lived to the west, they described the people as "those who live near the snaking river." The French shortened the word to *Sioux*.

Sitting Bull is credited with saying, "When I was a boy, the [Sioux] owned the world." Before the settlers came, the Dakota/Lakota/Nakota Nation roamed a vast territory encompassing much of what would later become Minnesota, North Dakota, South Dakota, northern Nebraska, eastern Wyoming, southeastern Montana, and north into Canada. Because of this large territory, the three dialects evolved along with other cultural differences as a result of distinct environments. The Dakota live east of the Missouri River, where the landscape is mostly small hills, lakes, and woodlands. The Lakota live in the plains west of the Missouri River, and the Nakota live along the river itself. Each of these environments offers unique challenges and requires different words and approaches to hunting, gathering, planting, medicines, and social and religious gatherings.

The Dakota/Lakota/Nakota Nation is comprised of seven bands. This alliance is referred to as the **Oceti Šakowiŋ** or Seven Council Fires. The following are the names of the Oceti Šakowiŋ:

Mdewakaŋtoŋwaŋ
The Spirit Lake People

Waȟpekute
The Shooters Among the Leaves People

Waȟpetoŋwaŋ
The People Dwelling Among the Leaves

THINGS TO LEARN IN THIS LESSON:

- The Great Sioux Nation
- Oceti Šakowiŋ, the Seven Council Fires
- Early European contact
- Treaties and government policy
- Modern accomplishments
- Other resources

THINKING AHEAD:

Think about a name you would choose for yourself as your new Dakota name for this class. Consider your personality, accomplishments or nicknames, or other traits that are important to you.

Sisitoŋwaŋ
People of the Fish Village(s)

Ihaŋktoŋwaŋ
Dwellers at the End

Ihaŋktoŋwaŋna
Little Dwellers at the End

Ti´toŋwaŋ
Dwellers on the Plains

The first four, the Mdewakaŋtoŋwaŋ, the Waȟpekute, the Waȟpetoŋwaŋ, and the Sisitoŋwaŋ, are the Santee or Dakota people. The Ihaŋktoŋwaŋ and the Ihaŋktoŋwaŋna are the Yankton or Nakota people. The Ti´toŋwaŋ are the Lakota or Teton people. The Lakota comprise the majority of the Dakota/Nakota/Lakota nation, and the Ti´toŋwaŋ are further divided into seven subgroups.

Early European Contact

During the first half of the 1800s, settlers began to invade the Dakota/Nakota/Lakota Nation's homelands. Between 1815 and 1858, the U.S. government, through force, negotiated treaties with the Sisseton Wahpeton bands. The Sisseton Wahpeton ceded their land in return for goods and cash. They were then moved to reservations and underwent enforced acculturation. They were required to abandon their own culture and language. Despite being a deeply spiritual people who honored **Wakaŋtaŋka**, the Great Spirit, in their daily lives, they were viewed as pagans. Missionaries were sent to convert them to Christianity.

To understand the Dakota people and their language, a little more history must be learned, beginning with the initial contact with missionaries and followed by government policy that has influenced Dakota language and culture.

The Missionary Era occurred in the early 1800s, and two prominent missionaries of this time were brothers Samuel W. and Gideon H. Pond, whose philosophy was that Indians were a diminishing race and as many as possible should be saved. Their efforts included developing knowledge about the Dakota people and language. The language and cultural barriers were the largest hurdles to bringing about mass conversion.

In 1833, the Pond brothers undertook the task of learning the Dakota language. To aid them, they developed an adapted English alphabet for writing Dakota. This same alphabet is used today for writing Dakota. By spring of 1835, both brothers had made great progress in daily Dakota conversation. They began to think in the language and, in doing so, began to understand the Dakota culture better as well.

Treaties and Government Policy

The U.S. government through treaties and various policies and acts has had an enormous impact on the languages of indigenous peoples. We will briefly mention a couple examples in this very complex field of study.

- 1867 Treaty with the Sisseton Wahpeton bands (See Appendix)
- Assimilationist Policy (1890–1934)

The Assimilationist Policy enacted the most destructive years of U.S. government actions toward native populations. Traditional tribal governments were inhibited from operating. The prohibition of self-governance resulted in total economic and political dependence of the Dakota people on the Bureau of Indian Affairs (BIA). The government plan was to redefine and assimilate all American Indian peoples into dominant European society and to abolish reservations. Therefore, they separated Dakota children from their families and sent them to boarding schools. The goals of these boarding schools, such as the one in Morris, Minnesota, were to enlighten and show the Dakota people the path to joining U.S. society. Unfortunately, boarding schools had terrible repercussions for indigenous peoples. Because children were forbidden to speak their language and received severe consequences for disobeying the rules, generations of Dakota people lost the ability to speak Dakota. As you will learn, a loss of the language leads also to a loss of culture, since the two are tightly intertwined.

From 1934 to 1955, the Dakota people continued to feel the strong effects of the prohibition against speaking their language and practicing their religion. Dakota studies were not permitted in public schools until the 1970s. At the time, no formal research or written materials were developed documenting the Dakota's language, history, or culture.

In 1972, the Sisseton Wahpeton tribe, under the Indian Education Act of 1972 (P.L. 92-318), applied for funding to develop a bilingual/bicultural education program. Beginning in 1975, public schools around the reservation allowed the Dakota language and culture to be taught. In 1978, the American Indian Religious Freedom Act granted American Indians the right to practice their own religion, live their own cultures, and speak their own language.

Modern Accomplishments

Today, the Sisseton Wahpeton Dakota Nation, renamed from the Sisseton Wahpeton Sioux Tribe, has more than 11,000 tribal members. The Sisseton Wahpeton Dakota Nation struggles with the social ills of the times, like diabetes, chemical abuse, teenage pregnancy, suicide, unemployment, and poverty. There is no easy fix, but many believe that if the people can return to a more traditional lifestyle their situations will improve.

The Sisseton Wahpeton Dakota Nation's many recent accomplishments include the following:

- Sisseton Wahpeton College, originally a community college, now a college offering associate degrees in twenty-two programs and certificates in five others
- Tribal daycare
- Constructing a new, modern school facility housing grades K-12
- Creating a new skating rink
- Creating a community center at Old Agency
- Dakota Western, a plastic bag and plastic products manufacturing plant
- Dakota Pride Treatment Center for chemical dependency
- Enemy Swim Day school

The Sisseton Wahpeton Dakota Nation also has three casinos: the Dakota Sioux Casino near Watertown, South Dakota, the Connection Casino near Sisseton on I-29, and the Dakota Magic Casino near Hankinson, North Dakota. The Dakota Magic Casino displays seven torches in front, symbolizing the seven council fires of the Dakota/Lakota/Nakota Nation.

Many people work to create a future for the Dakota people—a future that does not forget the traditions of the past.

OTHER RESOURCES

The following are suggested readings, videos, and websites. The content is not endorsed by the authors: they are simply resources for you to explore. When reading and learning, ask yourself the following questions:

- Who is the author(s)?
- What is his/her motivation for writing or creating the book, video, or website?
- Is she/he trustworthy or credible?

Remember! There are many myths and untruths about the Dakota and Native Americans in general. *Always* question the source, use your own judgment, and, if possible, verify the information with an elder.

SUGGESTED READINGS

The Soul of the Indian: An Interpretation by Charles Eastman

The Dakota Sioux in Canada by Gontran Laviolette

American Indian Tribal Governments by Sharon O'Brien

Speaking of Indians by Ella Deloria

Sacred Language: The Nature of Supernatural Discourse in Lakota by William K. Powers

Ehanna Woyakapi: History and Culture of the Sisseton Wahpeton Sioux Tribe of South Dakota by the Sisseton Wahpeton Sioux Tribe

Legends of the Mighty Sioux compiled by the South Dakota Writers' Project and illustrated by Oscar Howe

History of the Santee Sioux: United States Indian Policy on Trial by Roy W. Meyers

Kinsmen of Another Kind: Dakota-White Relations in the Upper Mississippi Valley, 1650–1862 by Gary Clayton Anderson

The Mystic Warriors of the Plains by Thomas E. Mails

Hau Kóla!: The Plains Indian Collection of the Haffenreffer Museum of Anthropology by Barbara A. Hail

Joseph N. Nicollet on the Plains and Prairies: The Expeditions of 1838–39, with Journals, Letters, and Notes on the Dakota Indians translated and edited by Edmund C. Bray and Martha Coleman Bray

SUGGESTED VIDEOS

The Dakota Conflict, Twin Cities Public Television

Dakota Exile, Twin Cities Public Television

In the Whiteman's Image

In Whose Honor? Indian Mascots in U.S. Sports

Live and Remember

SUGGESTED WEBSITES

codetalkers.org

www.census.gov

www.earthskyweb.com

www.nmai.si.edu

www.dlncoalition.org/home.htm

http://publicagenda.org/reports/walking-mile-first-step-toward-mutual-understanding

EXERCISES FOR LESSON ONE

1. Describe your current understanding and knowledge of the Dakota language.

2. Define *dialect*.

3. What are the three divisions of the Great Sioux Nation?

4. Why is the Siouan language divided into these three linguistic groups? Give other examples of languages that began as one language but eventually evolved into one or more dialects and then separate languages.

5. List the bands that comprise the Oceti Šakowiŋ.

6. Write about the appropriateness of *Sioux* to identify the Dakota/Lakota/Nakota Nation. Why do you suppose this misnomer has been perpetuated so long? Why wasn't their true name(s) used in the first place?

7. Why did the government prohibit the Dakota from speaking their language? What was the ultimate goal? Explain the logic and motivation of these acts and policies.

8. What effects did the boarding schools have on American Indians? Can we still see these effects today?

9. Why is saving the language important to the Dakota people? Research other indigenous cultures to determine what they are doing to successfully preserve their languages.

Read the treaty in the Appendix (page 93) and answer the following questions.

10. What is the intent of each article?

11. What did the Sisseton Wahpeton Dakota people cede in this agreement?

12. What did the U.S. government cede or promise in this agreement?

13. What do you think of the language used? For example, "Congress will, in its own discretion, from time to time make such appropriations as may be deemed requisite . . ."

14. What kinds of "allowances" does Congress make in terms of health, housing, food, hunting, clothing, or education?

15. How have those allowances been honored from 1867 until the present day?

16. What kind of impact do you think these treaties and allowances made on the Dakotas' way of life?

17. Who signed this treaty? What kind of authority did each of these individuals have?

18. Find a different treaty of your choice. Present it to the class noting similarities and differences between the treaty you've chosen and the Sisseton Wahpeton Treaty. Look for these treaties in your library or via the Internet. This website may be helpful in your search: http://digital.library.okstate.edu/kappler/Vol2/Toc.htm

19. Choose a topic relating to the Dakota people and write a paper on it using these instructions:

FORMAT: The paper must be at least three pages long, double spaced, with a standard 12-point font and one-inch margins. Use at least three credible resources and cite them on a separate "Works Cited" page in acceptable format. Resources can be credible books, magazines, videos, websites, and people.

Here are some broad topic suggestions, but you are free to write about anything as long as the topic relates to the Dakota people.

- Siouan linguistic divisions
- Siouan cultural divisions
- Dakota religion
- Wacipis or powwows
- Ceremonies
- Cultural aspects
- Dakota traditional food
- Dakota traditional clothing
- Dakota traditional family structure
- Dakota and other tribal relations
- U.S. government and the Dakota people
- Current Dakota issues like politics, health care, education
- Dakota economics, past, present, or both
- Dakota people in history or current events
- Dakota artists, authors, or actors
- Dakota/Lakota/Nakota Nations as portrayed in movies and/or books
- The U.S.–Dakota War of 1862
- Land occupied by the Dakota/Lakota/Nakota before and/or after European settlers arrived
- Dakota or American Indians in the U.S. military

20. Despite years of oppression, Native people across the world have excelled in many areas, becoming successful authors, artists, and filmmakers and achieving notoriety in the fields of science and business. Choose a notable individual and write a one-page description of his or her background (including obstacles encountered) and accomplishments.

Lesson Two: Dakota Alphabet

THINGS TO LEARN IN THIS LESSON:

- Letters of the Dakota alphabet
- Sounds of the Dakota alphabet
- Word accent
- Sentence shape

LETTER	SOUND	DAKOTA	ENGLISH
a	father	ate	father
b	boy	bdo	potato
c	chore	canku	road
ĉ	(exploded)	ciĉu	to give you
d	day	do	It is so.
e	they	ŝak´pe	six
g	give	ŝuŋgmanitu	wolf
ġ	(guttural)	hoġan	fish
h	hello	haŋpi	juice
ĥ	(guttural)	wo´wiĥa	funny
i	machine	ina	mother
k	kite	ka´ta	hot
ķ	(exploded)	ķa	and
m	mouse	mni	water
n	new	nina	very
ŋ	(nasal) ink	taŋ´ka	large
o	go	to	blue
p	party	pa	head
Þ	(exploded)	Þo	fog/mist
¢	(exploded)	¢a	and
s	see	ska	white
ŝ	shower	ŝi´ca	bad
t	town	tonana	few
ŧ	(exploded)	ŧe	dead
u	choose	du´ta	red/scarlet
w	warn	wo´wapi	book
y	yellow	yam´ni	three
z	zebra	ma´zaska	money
ż	azure	pe´tiżaŋżaŋ	lamp

Dakota Sounds

In the Dakota language, the alphabet sounds that are presented *never* change! Unlike the English alphabet, each Dakota letter sounds the same in every word. This means that the language is phonetic and every word should be easy to sound out.

Accent

The stress point or accent of most words is on the second syllable, unless noted when introduced in the book. Be careful when observing this rule: changing the accent can change the meaning of the word. For example, *ma´ġa* means "garden or field," while *maġa´* means "goose."

Remember, the accent of most words is on the *second syllable* and so will not be marked. If the word *begins with "wo,"* the accent will be on the first syllable. When the word does not follow these two rules, an accent mark [´] will follow the accented syllable. *The accent mark will appear on the word only in the lesson where the word first appears and in the glossaries.* After that, it is your responsibility to remember the correct accent!

Sentence Shape

The shape of the sentences, while very melodic, is usually downward sloping. While English sentences traditionally sound very bouncy, with the sounds of the words going up and down, Dakota sentences usually have a downward step shape.

English sentence shape:

Dakota sentence shape:

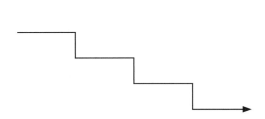

EXERCISES FOR LESSON TWO

1. Study the description of the sounds and practice making each letter sound. Remember the sounds *never* change, so learn them well now.

2. List five English words with the same sound as each of the vowels in the Dakota alphabet.

3. List differences between the English alphabet and the Dakota alphabet.

4. Where is the stress or accent within the Dakota sentences and words?

5. Draw the shape of an English sentence.

6. Draw the shape of a Dakota sentence.

7. Think about all the different sounds in the English language and try to remember how difficult it was to remember when the sounds changed. For instance, the English *c* may sound like the first *c* in *cancer* or it may sound like an *s* as in the second *c* in *cancer*. This does not happen in Dakota. How will this make the language easier or harder to learn?

Lesson Three:
Dakota Names

THINGS TO LEARN IN THIS LESSON:

- Basic words to describe people

- Immediate Dakota family

- Dakota names and naming ceremony

People and Family

We will start by learning the most basic words for the people around us. Note that sometimes *wicaṡta* is abbreviated as **wica** and *wiŋ´yaŋ* is abbreviated as **wiŋ.**

Wicaṡta	man
Wiŋ´yaŋ	woman
Siceca	child
Hokṡina/da	boy
Wiciŋyaŋna	girl

Mitakuye: Immediate Family

Kuŋ´ṡi	paternal grandmother
Tuŋkaŋṡi	paternal grandfather
Uŋci	maternal grandmother
Uŋkaŋ	maternal grandfather
Ate	father
Ina	mother
Ciŋkṡi	son
Cuŋkṡi	daughter

Dakota Names

BOYS	BIRTH ORDER	GIRLS
Caske	first-born	Winona
Hepaŋ	second-born	Ha´paŋ
Hepi	third-born	Ha´pstiŋ
Ca´taŋ	fourth-born	Waŋ´ske
Hake	fifth-born	Wihake

The Dakota children of each family are initially named using the same five names based on the birth order of the child. The birth order is separate for boys and girls. For instance, if a family has four children, a girl, a boy, a boy, and a girl, the first-born girl is Winona. The boy, although he is the second child to be born, is the first-born son, so his name is Caske. The other two children would be Hepan and Ha´pan. The parents can name children born after the fifth child as they wish. They can be named for the time of day or the season in which they are born, or they can be given the name of a dead or elderly relative.

NOTE:

Different dialects may use different word endings. In this book, variations are shown with a slash mark, as in *hokṡina/da* on this page.

Dakota Naming Ceremony

The Dakota naming ceremony connects the newly named with the past, the future, nature, and the spirit world. The newly named is given either a name from an ancestor or a name based on his or her characteristics. Hereafter, the newly named will be known by this name rather than the birth-order name.

The one being named makes the following obligatory preparations:

- Select a ceremony site or location
- Select a spiritual person to perform the ceremony
- Send out invitations
- Gather the elements of the ceremony, which include the following: four cherry branches, large tobacco ties representing the sacred colors of yellow, white, red, and blue, a large red tobacco tie to hang out on a cottonwood tree, and singers to sing the name-giving song.

Once a name is given by ceremony, the name is shouted to the four directions, to the above and below, and to the guests. This practice introduces the new person to all the elements. After the ceremony, the person's family provides a feast of traditional foods.

The last act of the ceremony is the giveaway. People are called to receive gifts from the relatives of the newly named. People run with joy to claim their gifts, and it is a great honor to be included. This event is the most important of the naming ceremony because it creates and strengthens kinship bonding.

EXERCISES FOR LESSON THREE

1. A Dakota family has three girls and two boys. What are the children's names?

2. What if they later have five more children, three more girls and two more boys? What will they name these children?

3. Why do you think the Dakota name their children this way?

4. Create a picture collage of a family, labeling each family member as appropriate. Present it to the class. Practice the pronunciation of each word and review Lesson Two as needed.

5. What kinds of qualities might a person be named for?

6. What kinds of preparations are undertaken by the person being named?

7. What kinds of trees are used in the naming ceremony?

Underline the stressed syllable in each of the Dakota words listed.

8. Wi ca ŝta

9. Ciŋ kŝi

10. Hok ŝi na/da

11. I na

12. Hap stiŋ

13. Uŋ ci

14. Cuŋ kŝi

15. Tuŋ kaŋ ŝi

16. Ha ke

17. Ha paŋ

18. A te

19. He pi

20. He paŋ

21. Waŋ ske

22. Wiŋ yaŋ

23. Kuŋ ŝi

Lesson Four: Beginning Conversation

THINGS TO LEARN IN THIS LESSON:

- Beginning conversational sentences

- Different male/female responses and words

- Asking a question

Start by learning some basic conversational sentences. Do not worry about the exact meaning or conjugation of all the words yet: these sentences are simply warm-up phrases for you to memorize. Also note that conversation sometimes has different responses for males and females. Be sure to choose the correct response! Finally, to ask a question, add the word *he* to the end of the sentence. Remember that Dakota sentences always go "downhill" (see Lesson Two), so the *he* is very important!

	MALE	FEMALE
Hello or Yes	Hau	Haŋ
It is so.	Do.	Ye.
I am here.	Wahi do/ye.	
How are you?	To´ked yauŋ he?	
I am fine.	Taŋyaŋ wauŋ do/ye.	
I am tired.	Miye wamatuka do/ye.	
Good day.	Aŋpetu wašte.	
I like to speak Dakota.	Dakota ia waštewadaka do/ye.	
What are you called?	To´ked eniciyapi he?	
I am called _____.	_____ emakiyapi do/ye.	
What is his/her name?	To´ked eciyapi he?	
S/he is called _____.	_____ eciyapi do/ye.	
Where do you live?	To´kiya yati he?	
I live _____.	_____ ed wati do/ye.	
Where does s/he live?	To´kiya ti he?	
S/he lives here.	_____ ded ti do/ye.	
Thank you.	Pidamaya do/ye.	
Be well/Be good.	Taŋyaŋ uŋ wo.	
Does s/he go to school?	Wayawa he?	
S/he goes to school at _____.	_____ ed wayawa do/ye.	
Does s/he work or no?	Nakun, ȟtani kaiš ȟtani šni he?	
S/he works.	Ȟtani do/ye.	
Where does s/he work?	Tukte ed ȟtani he?	
S/he works at _____.	_____ ed ȟtani ye.	
Good health (after a sneeze)	Zani wašte ye/do.	

Translate these English sentences to Dakota.

1. Hello. (Female)

2. How are you?

3. I am fine (It is so).

4. I am tired (It is so).

5. What is your name?

6. Where does he work?

7. Where do you live?

8. I like to speak Dakota.

9. I am called _____.

10. Be good/well.

11. Where does he live?

12. I live _____.

13. He works at the SuperValu.

Translate these Dakota sentences. If possible, note whether a male or female is speaking.

14. Wowiȟa wiŋ eciyapi ye.

15. Morris ded wati do.

16. Pidamaya do.

17. Taŋyaŋ wauŋ ye.

18. Aŋpetu waŝte.

19. Haŋ, North Dakota State University ed wayawa ye.

20. Tokiya ti he?

21. Miye wamatuka ye.

22. Hau.

23. Wahi ye.

24. Toked yauŋ he?

25. Practice a beginning conversation with a partner for ten minutes. Pay close attention to the proper sounds. Review Lesson Two as needed. Be very conscious of your vocalization as you are learning.

Lesson Five:
Numbers and Colors

**THINGS TO LEARN
IN THIS LESSON:**

- Numbers

- Words that describe quantity

- Colors

Numbers

The first ten numbers are the most important to memorize, because the rest of the numbers are derived from them. Here is a listing of the numbers 1 through 20, and by tens from 20 to 100.

1	Waŋ´ca
2	Noŋ´pa
3	Ya´mni
4	To´pa
5	Za´ptaŋ
6	Ŝa´kpe
7	Ŝakowiŋ
8	Ŝahdoġaŋ
9	Napciŋwaŋka
10	Wikcemna
11	Ake waŋži
12	Ake noŋpa
13	Ake yamni
14	Ake topa
15	Ake zaptaŋ
16	Ake ŝakpe
17	Ake ŝakowiŋ
18	Ake ŝahdoġaŋ
19	Ake napciŋwaŋka
20	Wikcemna noŋpa
30	Wikcemna yamni
40	Wikcemna topa
50	Wikcemna zaptaŋ
60	Wikcemna ŝakpe
70	Wikcemna ŝakowiŋ
80	Wikcemna ŝahdoġaŋ
90	Wikcemna napciŋwaŋka
100	Wanzi

The words for the teens are prefaced with the word **ake,** which means "again." Notice that the word for "one" in "eleven" is *waŋži* instead of *waŋ´ca. Waŋ´ca* appears only once for the first number "one." After the first use, the word for "one" is *waŋži.* Waŋži is also used when referring to *one* as an adjective when talking about how many, such as one book or one dog. For counting in multiples of ten, the Dakota word *wikcemna noŋpa* means two tens, *wikcemna* (meaning ten) and *noŋpa* (meaning two). Thirty is three tens, *wikcemna yamni,* and so on. To count between multiples of ten, use the Dakota word **som.** *Som* is a contraction of *saŋ´pa,* which means "more." For example, twenty-six is **wikcemna noŋpa som šakpe** and fifty-five is **wikcemna zaptaŋ som zaptaŋ.**

Other words can describe quantities without using a specific number. The words for quantities are

Waniĉa	none
Waŋ´ca	once
Owasin	all
O´ta	lots/many
Saŋ´pa	more
Oŋġe	some
Ta´kuna šni	nothing
To´nana	few

Colors

Dakota is a wonderfully descriptive and literal language. Here are some of the most common Dakota colors. Notice how some of the colors "make up" another color. For example, the word for the color orange is made with a combination of either red and yellow or yellow and brown.

Du´ta	red/scarlet
Ŝa	red
Ŝazi	orange
Zi´ġi	orange
Zi	yellow
Watoto	green
Zito	green
To	blue
Tostaŋ	purple
Ġi	brown
Sa´pa	black
Ħo´ta	gray
Ska	white

Wo´yawa means "a counting" in Dakota. Put your counting and translation skills to the test with the following exercises. Don't let the long words intimidate you! Determine each word that makes up the number first and then put them together.

1. 45

2. 89

3. 10

4. 4

5. 14

6. 1

7. 31

8. 52

9. 67

10. 100

11. 10

12. 19

13. 5

14. 77

15. 28

16. 93

17. Ake šakpe

18. Wikcemna topa

19. Ta´kuna šni

20. Šakowiŋ

21. Wikcemna napciwaŋka som napciŋwaŋka

22. Ake šahdoġaŋ

23. Ota

24. Yamni

25. Wikcemna šakowiŋ som zaptaŋ

26. Wikcemna noŋpa som waŋži

27. Opawiŋġe

28. Wikcemna topa som šahdoġaŋ

Match the following:

29. Zi   a. Black

30. To   b. White

31. Ska   c. Blue

32. Sapa   d. Red/scarlet

33. Duta   e. Yellow

Write the correct answer in Dakota words.

34. $4 + 10$

35. 8×5

36. $87 - 14$

37. $44 \div 11$

38. 9×3

39. $75 - 25$

Do the math and write the answer as both a number and the correct Dakota word.

40. Noŋpa $\times$ zaptaŋ

41. Ake šahdoġaŋ $-$ šahdoġaŋ

42. Wikcemna noŋpa $\div$ topa

43. Yamni $+$ napciŋwaŋka

44. Šakpe $\times$ šakowiŋ

45. Wikcemna šahdoġaŋ som waŋži $\div$ napciŋwaŋka

46. Wan´ca $\times$ opawiŋġe

Write the Dakota name for each color.

47. White

48. Purple

49. Brown

50. Gray

51. Green

52. Blue

53. Black

54. Orange

55. Yellow

56. Red

Translate the following:

57. Once

58. More

59. All

60. Few

61. Nothing

62. Some

63. Lots

64. Saŋpa

65. Ȟoʹta

66. Ska

67. Duʹta

68. None

Woonspe Ŝakpe: Simple Verb Conjugation

THINGS TO LEARN IN THIS LESSON:

- Simple verb conjugation

- New simple verbs

- Translating from Dakota to English

First of all, notice that the title bar has changed! Instead of reading "Lesson Six," it now reads "Woonspe Ŝakpe." **Wo´onspe** means "lesson," and of course the lesson number is now in Dakota as well. The lesson titles that follow will appear in Dakota.

Simple Verb Conjugation

Let's begin by thinking about English sentences and grammar. We will start with the most basic concepts and work our way up, building on each concept.

The most basic English sentence consists of a subject and a verb. The subject of a sentence is a word that names the person or thing about which something is said. The verb is the word used to express action or a state of being. A simple example of this is "John wants." *John* is the subject and *wants* is the verb.

In many languages, the subject is incorporated into the verb form as a subjective pronoun. One can use a subject in a sentence, but it is not necessary. The Dakota language incorporates a subjective pronoun into the verb form. Dakota has an additional verb form called the "dual number." It consists of the person speaking and the person spoken to: we two, the two of us, you and I.

In order to form verbs in Dakota, one must add to the root verb. The root verb is usually listed in the dictionary in the third person singular (S/He/It) form. We will begin with the simple root verb *ciŋ,* which means "s/he/it wants." We have highlighted the verb root in the conjugated forms to make it easier for you to see how it works. The words on the following page conjugate in the same manner. Note the subtle yet important difference between the two verbs *ti* and *ni. Ti* means "lives somewhere" and *ni* means "has life" or "is alive"!

SIMPLE ROOT VERB CONJUGATION PATTERN			
		You and I	**Uŋ**____
I	**Wa**____	We	**Uŋ**____**pi**
You	**Ya**____	You all	**Ya**____**pi**
S/He/It	____	They	____**pi**

Take careful note of the conjugation pattern. Many verbs and later other parts of speech will follow the same pattern.

Memorize the pattern now!

		CIŊ (S/HE/IT WANTS)	
		You and I want.	Uŋciŋ
I want.	Waciŋ	We want.	Uŋciŋpi
You want.	Yaciŋ	You all want.	Yaciŋpi
S/He/It wants.	Ciŋ	They want.	Ciŋ´pi

		TI (S/HE/IT LIVES [SOMEWHERE])	
		You and I live.	Uŋti
I live.	Wati	We live.	Uŋtipi
You live.	Yati	You all live.	Yatipi
S/He/It lives.	Ti	They live.	Ti´pi

		NI (S/HE/IT LIVES/IS ALIVE)	
		You and I live.	Uŋni
I live.	Wani	We live.	Uŋnipi
You live.	Yani	You all live.	Yanipi
S/He/It lives.	Ni	They live.	Ni´pi

		KUWA (S/HE/IT FOLLOWS, FLIRTS, CHASES, HUNTS, OR PURSUES)	
		You and I follow.	Uŋkuwa
I follow.	Wakuwa	We follow.	Uŋkuwapi
You follow.	Yakuwa	You all follow.	Yakuwapi
S/He/It follows.	Kuwa	They follow.	Kuwapi

		KAMNA (S/HE/IT EARNS)	
		You and I earn.	Uŋkamna
I earn.	Wakamna	We earn.	Uŋkamnapi
You earn.	Yakamna	You all earn.	Yakamnapi
S/He/It earns.	Kamna	They earn.	Kamnapi

New Verbs

Here are more simple verbs to learn. The verbs are listed in their third-person singular form.

"Somewhere" represents a placeholder for whatever specific place or prepositional phrase will be used. For example, to finish the sentence, one might say "She lives in town": "in town" would be the "somewhere" in that sentence. "Something" also represents a placeholder for whatever specific direct object will be used. For example, to finish the sentence, one might say "He cuts up the potato": "the potato" would be the "something" in that sentence. As you learn more words, they can replace the generic "something" or "somewhere."

Da	S/He/It asks for (something)
Hde	S/He/It leaves/sets out for home
Hdi	S/He/It returns/comes back
Ḳa	S/He/It digs up (something)
Kacoco	S/He/It stirs or mixes up (something)
Kaĥapa	S/He/It drives (something)
Kaksa	S/He/It cuts (something)
Kaptaŋyaŋ	S/He/It turns or flips (with an instrument)
Kipaŋ	S/He/It calls (to someone)
Kipazo	S/He/It shows or points out (one's own item)
Ḱu	S/He/It gives (something)
Ŝa	S/He/It shouts or yells
Ŝkaŋ	S/He/It moves about
Ŝkata	S/He/It plays

Translating from Dakota to English

Because the Dakota words have very specific meanings, they do not always translate into one word in English. For example, *ciŋ* means "want," but *kipaŋ* means "to call (to someone)." The extra English words are needed to clarify the Dakota verb. *Kipaŋ* is distinct from a verb that may mean "to call (over to oneself)" or "to call (for something)." In the following exercises, the English translations are longer due to the required verb phrase translations.

EXERCISES FOR WOONSPE ŜAKPE

1. Is a separate subject necessary when speaking Dakota? Why or why not?

2. What is a root verb?

3. List and define the verb forms that can be conjugated. For example, *I* is first person singular and the Dakota form prefixes the root verb with *wa*.

4. What does "dual number" mean?

5. Define and conjugate the Dakota root verb *ciŋ*. Create a "conjugation box" as on pages 19 and 20.

6. Define and conjugate the Dakota word for "S/He/It digs up (something)."

Translate the following English sentences to Dakota. Because the subject is incorporated into the verb, the sentences will be just one word.

7. We return.

8. They dig up something.

9. I stir.

10. He cuts something.

11. You and I earn.

12. You all call to someone.

13. You stir.

14. I give something.

15. You and I move about.

16. You all live.

17. He mixes up.

18. You all come back.

19. You and I cut something.

20. You all turn or flip with an instrument.

21. We stir.

22. You give something.

23. You and I yell.

24. You all mix up something.

25. You and I ask for something.

26. I live.

27. You dig up something.

28. They mix.

29. You all earn.

30. They turn or flip with an instrument.

31. You point out your own item.

32. You and I pursue.

33. We shout.

34. They play.

35. You and I want.

36. They set out for home.

37. You return.

38. She digs up something.

39. We drive.

40. You all cut something.

41. You call to someone.

42. You and I give something.

43. They move about.

44. You live.

45. We want.

46. I leave.

47. It comes back.

48. You and I dig up something.

49. You all drive.

50. They cut something.

51. You flip with an instrument (like a spatula).

52. You and I point out something of our own.

53. We give something.

54. You all chase.

55. He lives.

56. You all want.

57. We dig up something.

58. They drive.

59. You earn.

60. You and I call someone.

61. They hunt.

62. I shout.

63. He plays.

64. They want.

65. I ask for something.

66. She leaves.

67. We come.

68. You all dig up something.

69. You cut something.

70. He earns.

71. You all point out your own item.

72. You yell.

73. We live.

Now translate the following one-word Dakota sentences into English. The English translation will be two or more words. Be sure to write out the verb phrase if there is one—be specific!

74. Yada.

75. Uŋhde.

76. Yakaȟapa.

77. Uŋkaptaŋyaŋpi.

78. Kipazopi.

79. Yakuwa.

80. Ŝa.

81. Uŋŝkatapi.

82. Yaciŋ.

83. Da.

84. Uŋhdepi.

85. Uŋkacoco.

86. Kaȟapa.

87. Uŋkamnapi.

88. Kipaŋpi.

89. Wakipazo.

90. Kuwa.

91. Uŋŝkaŋpi.

92. Yaŝkatapi.

93. Nipi.

94. Ciŋ.

95. Yahdapi.

96. Hdipi.

97. Uŋkaȟapa.

98. Uŋkaksapi.

99. Wakipaŋ.

100. Ku̇.

101. Yaŝkanpi.

102. Wani.

103. Uŋdapi.

104. Wahdi.

105. Kamnapi.

106. Wakaptaŋyaŋ.

107. Kipazo.

108. Uŋkuwapi.

109. Yaŝapi.

110. Waŝkata.

111. Yadapi.

112. Yahdi.

113. Wakamna.

114. Kipaŋ.

115. Ŝapi.

116. Waŝkaŋ.

117. Yaŝkata.

118. Dapi.

119. Yahde.

120. Hdi.

121. Wakuwa.

122. Ŝkan.

123. Uŋŝkata.

124. Uŋni.

125. Wakaksa.

126. Kaptaŋyaŋ.

127. Uŋkipazopi.

128. Yakupi.

129. Yaŝkaŋ.

130. Uŋni.

131. Uŋhdi.

132. Wakaȟapa.

133. Uŋkaptaŋyaŋ.

134. Uŋkipaŋpi.

135. Ku´pi.

136. Waǩa

If you've completed this lesson, you're doing great! Yes, it's long, but it's meant to make you *very* familiar with the simple conjugation techniques. This exercise will help a lot in future lessons as the conjugation schemes become more complicated.

Woonspe Ŝakowiŋ: Dakota Purpose

THINGS TO LEARN IN THIS LESSON:

- The purpose of the Dakota language

- Four major purposes of learning Dakota

The Purpose of the Dakota Language

Because language defines how a person thinks and exists, the old Dakota language spoken by the ancestors of the Dakota people was a beautiful way to communicate. The language provided a true sense of belonging to the Great Mystery, the Created order of things, the Universe, Mother Earth, animals, wingeds, swimmers, crawlers, and the other two-leggeds.

All the Dakota people were born into a vision, and all knew who they were. The Dakota kinship system provided a tie to all things big or small, seen or unseen, and through this system, all things held a great purpose in Creation.

Because of this vast kinship system, Dakota people hardly ever called each other by first name but greeted one another by a relative-kinship term. If there was no kinship system established for an individual, one was created by adoption into the family. Once adopted into the family, the kinship extended to personal relationships and the greater relationships of the spirits, animals, and other Created beings.

Eli Taylor, a Dakota elder, describes the Dakota language as follows (words in brackets added for clarification): "Our native language embodies a value system about how we ought to live and relate to each other. It gives a name to relations among kin, to roles and responsibilities among family members, to ties with the broader clan group . . . there [are] no English words for these relationships because [the European] social and family life is different from the [Dakota's family life]. If you destroy [the Dakota] language, you not only break down these relationships but you destroy other aspects of the [Dakota] way of life and culture, especially those that describe man's connection to nature, the Great Spirit, and the order of things. Without the language, the Dakota will cease to exist as a separate people."

The Four Purposes of Learning Dakota

The four purposes of learning the Dakota language are as follows:

Internalized information. Through listening and repeating stories, a person comes to understand the wonders of life. Unique information filtered through lessons teach about all things—creation, origin accounts, social science, psychology, and existence. This information, which is passed to each generation, instills the importance of values, concepts, and proper social expectations and behavior.

Ground of being. The Dakota language explains all of life through its dependence on a chain of relationships. The Dakota language is intricately linked to the joy of living and how the Dakota people are intimately related to each other and all of Creation.

History. The Dakota language, and the stories that belong to it, bring events from the past to life for the listener. The detail of the language explains the what, how, and who of the event.

Traditions and customs. The Dakota language and kinship relationships teach proper social behavior and the consequences of improper action. They also teach about the relationship of an individual to the social system as dictated by tradition, customs, and the observance of roles within one's family, community, tribe, extended bands, and nations.

Aside from these four generalized functions of the Dakota language, there are also more specific ways that the Dakota language defines the life of the Dakota people.

The Dakota language defines the following:

Cultural relationships. The Dakota language provides specialized names to each member of the family.

Cultural ties. The Dakota language defines the kinships of families, extended families, clans, and tribes and the roles and responsibilities to each other as a cooperative-communal clan.

Teachings. The Dakota language teaches all the Dakota about ethics, roles, responsibilities, behavioral and role expectations, and values.

Status and belonging. The Dakota language helps define an individual's family heritage and status within his or her family unit, clan, tribe, or nation.

Spiritual relationships. The Dakota language defines and teaches the human connection to every being within the Creation story and the ordering of all Creation. This includes Wakaŋtaŋka, **maka** (earth), and the other Creation spirits.

In short, the Dakota language defines how a person exists within the psychological, physical, social, and spiritual aspects of the Dakota world.

Woonspe Ŝahdoġan: Sentence Structure

THINGS TO LEARN IN THIS LESSON:

- Vocabulary
- Connecting words
- Basic rules for writing sentences
- Creating simple sentences
- Function words
- Plural forms
- Negatives
- Multiple descriptors
- Placement of a direct object

Vocabulary

This lesson begins with some new vocabulary words. These are nouns that you can begin to build sentences with. Remember that words beginning with *wo* are accented on the *first* syllable and that these accents will not be marked.

Ŝuŋ´ka	dog
Iŋmu	cat
Iŋmuŝuŋka	cat
Hoġaŋ	fish
Aŋpaohotoŋna	chicken
Ŝuŋ´kawakaŋ	horse
Ŝuŋtaŋka	horse
Ta´ĥca	deer
Ta´ĥiŋca	deer
Wo´wapi	letter or book
Mini	water
Wo´yute	food
I´yeciŋkaiyopte	car
Wa´ta	boat
Ti´pi	dwelling
Caŋ´akaŋyaŋkapi	chair
Wa´hnawotapi	table
Pe´tiżaŋżaŋ	lamp
Bdo	potato
Ma´zaska	money
Wahaŋpi	soup
Makawamduŝkadaŋ	earthworm
Miniĥoha/Miniĥuha	fabric
Wo´wapiska	paper

Connecting Words

These small words are ubiquitous in daily speech—the common *and, well,* and *but* that we cannot live without, even in Dakota.

Ḳa	and
Ġa	and
Ito	well
Tka	but

Basic Rules for Writing Sentences

Congratulations: now you know some verbs, adjectives (colors and numbers), and nouns. The next step is creating more complex sentences. Dakota sentences are constructed similarly to English sentences but with some differences. Pay attention to the examples. We have provided the Dakota sentence, a literal translation so you can see *which words are where,* and the English translation.

Creating very simple sentences: With a simple "bare bones" sentence consisting of a subject and a verb, the subject precedes the verb, as in English sentences. You already know that the "person" is incorporated into the verb. Let's use the familiar word *ciŋ* as an example.

Dakota sentence: Iŋmu ciŋ.
Literal translation: Cat (it) wants.
English translation: The cat wants.

Function words: One thing you will notice about Dakota is the absence of equivalent function words for the English words *a* and *the.* In Dakota, these words are *implied.* Note the literal translation of "The cat wants": simply "Iŋmu ciŋ." If you want to include more than one noun, you may do so by using the word *ḳa,* which means "and." If you are referring to more than one noun, subject, or object, you must create *a plural.*

Plural Forms: To create plurals, you must use quantity words, because the Dakota noun does not change to reflect number. You can use a number such as *noŋpa,* or you can use quantity words such as *oŋġe, owasin,* or *tonana.* (Review Lesson Five to refresh your memory.) When adding these words to the sentence, the quantity word follows the word it quantifies. An example of this kind of plural sentence is "Four cats want," which in Dakota would be "Iŋmu topa ciŋpi." Note the placement of the word *topa* (four) and the change in the verb form from the "S/He/It" form to the "They" form. Descriptive words follow the nouns they describe.

Dakota: Iŋmu topa ciŋpi.
Literal: Cat four (they) want.
English: Four cats want.

Negatives: To create a negative sentence or word, place the word **ŝŋi** after the word you want to negate. You can negate a verb or a noun by placing this word after it. For example, "No cat wants" would be "Inmu ŝŋi ciŋ."

Dakota: Iŋmu ŝŋi ciŋ.
Literal: Cat no (it) wants.
English: No cat wants.

To negate the verb, place *ŝŋi* after it. For example, "The cat does not want" would be "Inmu ciŋ ŝŋi."

Dakota:	Iŋmu ciŋ śni.
Literal:	Cat (it) wants not.
English:	The cat does not want.

More than one descriptive word: If more than one qualifying words describe a noun, they follow the noun in the inverse order that they would in English. For example, "The three black cats want" becomes "Iŋmu sapa yamni ciŋpi."

Dakota:	Iŋmu sapa yamni tipi.
Literal:	Cat black three (they) live.
English:	The three black cats live.

Placement of the direct object: A direct object is a person, place, or thing (a noun) that receives the action of the verb. If there is an object, the object is placed before the verb but after the noun and the noun's adjectives or modifiers. For example, "The white cat wants water" becomes "Iŋmu ska mini ciŋ."

Dakota:	Iŋmu ska mini ciŋ.
Literal:	Cat white water (it) wants.
English:	The white cat wants water.

Any adjectives or modifiers to the object are placed after the object but before the verb. For example, "The white cat wants two chickens" becomes "Iŋmu ska aŋpaohotoŋna noŋpa ciŋ."

Dakota:	Iŋmu ska aŋpaohotoŋna noŋpa ciŋ.
Literal:	Cat white chicken two (it) wants.
English:	The white cat wants two chickens.

EXERCISES FOR WOONSPE ŚAHDOĠAN

Underline the stressed syllable, then translate to English.

1. Wa haŋ pi

2. Ĥo ta

3. Wan ske

4. Kap taŋ yaŋ

5. To staŋ

6. Wa ta

7. Wo yu te

8. Wi ca śta

9. Tuŋ kaŋ śi

10. Ta ĥiŋ ca

11. Caŋ a kaŋ yaŋ ka pi

12. Ciŋ kśi

13. Wiŋ yaŋ

14. B do

15. Uŋ ci

16. Ti pi

17. A ke śa kpe

18. Iŋ mu

19. Mi ni

20. O ta

21. Aŋ pa o ho toŋ na

22. Ŝuŋ ka

23. Ca taŋ

24. Ma za ska

25. Wa hna wo ta pi

26. Ŝka ta

27. Ho ġaŋ

28. Wo wa pi ska

29. Ma ka wam du ŝka daŋ

30. O wa siŋ

31. To na na

32. Ŝuŋ ka wa kaŋ

33. Wa ciŋ

34. Pe ti żaŋ żaŋ

35. Ha pstin

36. A te

37. Waŋ ca

Answer the following by filling in the blank or writing in the space provided.

38. The most simple sentence consists of a _____ and a _____.

39. _____ and _____ do not have a Dakota equivalent.

40. Where are adjectives placed in the Dakota sentence?

41. What does the text mean by "literal translation"?

42. Describe the "accented syllable" rules you know so far and how unusual words are noted in this book.

True or false? If the sentence is false, rewrite it to be correct.

43. A direct object is a verb phrase.

44. To create a negative sentence or word, place the word *ŝni* after the word you want to negate.

45. The word for deer is *hoġaŋ*.

46. Words that begin with *wo* are accented on the last syllable.

47. *Waciŋ* is a Dakota word that means "I want."

48. The Dakota noun changes to create plurals by adding an *s*.

49. *Wakamna mazaska* translates as "You follow chickens."

50. Numbers and colors are not adjectives.

51. If there is more than one descriptive word, place one in front of and one behind the noun they are describing.

52. Adjectives to the direct object are placed after the object but before the verb.

Write these practice sentences in the three-sentence format. One has been done to show you how. The first set will be writing simple sentences.

53. Dakota translation: Cuŋkŝi ŝkata.

    Literal translation: Daughter (she) plays.

    English translation: Daughter plays.

54. English translation: The horse leaves for home.

55. English translation: The chicken wants.

56. English translation: The boy gives.

57. Dakota translation: Wicaŝta kuwa.

58. Dakota translation: Ŝuŋka ķa.

59. Dakota translation: Ina ķu.

60. Literal translation: Paternal grandmother (she) yells.

61. Literal translation: Woman (she) cuts something.

62. Literal translation: Father (he) drives.

63. English translation: The fish is alive.

Now practice writing plural sentences. Remember the noun does not change: you have to add a number word. The first one has been done for you.

64. Dakota translation: Siceca zaptaŋ śkatapi.

    Literal translation: Children five (they) play.

    English translation: The five children play.

65. English translation: Some horses move about.

66. English translation: Two chickens want.

67. English translation: Ten boys give something.

68. Dakota translation: Wicaśta ake noŋpa kuwapi.

69. Dakota translation: Śuŋka owasin kapi.

70. Dakota translation: Ina oŋġe kamna.

71. Literal translation: Mother some (they) earn.

72. Literal translation: Maternal grandfather few (they) yell.

73. Literal translation: Father more wants.

74. Dakota translation: Wowapi ska saŋpa wakaksa.

75. English translation: Thirty fish move about.

Practice putting multiple descriptors on the subject. The first one is done for you.

76. Dakota translation: Śuŋkawakaŋ ĥota wicemna śkatapi.

    Literal translation: Horse gray ten (they) play.

    English translation: Ten gray horses play.

77. English translation: Few yellow chickens come back.

78. English translation: Eight black dogs dig up ten earthworms.

79. Dakota translation: Iŋmu ska topa kuwapi.

80. Dakota translation: Hoġan to wikcemna śkanpi.

81. Literal translation: Deer brown twenty-five (they) have life.

Practice adding a direct object to the sentence. Remember that the direct object receives the action of the verb. The first one is done for you.

82. Dakota translation: Woyute waciŋ.

    Literal translation: Food (I) want.

    English translation: I want food.

83. English translation: You ask for water.

84. English translation: You and I dig up a potato.

85. English translation: I cut paper.

86. Dakota translation: Ta´ĥca kuwapi.

87. Dakota translation: Ma´zaska wakamna.

88. Dakota translation: Makawamduśkadaŋ waḳa.

89. Literal translation: Car (you) drive.

90. Literal translation: Chair (we) make.

91. Literal translation: Soup (she) stirs.

92. Dakota translation: Ina wakipaŋ.

Practice adding descriptors to the direct object. Continue writing the sentences in the three-sentence format.

93. English translation: I cut five brown potatoes.

94. English translation: They give thirty gray horses.

95. Dakota translation: Petiżaŋżaŋ tośtan wikcemna wada.

96. Dakota translation: Wa´hŋawotapi ġi wikcemna šakowiŋ som topa uŋku.

97. Literal translation: Cat chicken white five (it) chased.

Now practice multiple descriptors on both the subject and direct object. Remember in what order they are placed!

98. Dakota translation: Aŋpaohotoŋna owasin woyute wašte ciŋpi.

Literal translation: _____

English translation: All chickens want good food.

99. Dakota translation: _____

Literal translation: _____

English translation: Two daughters do not want four black dogs.

100. Dakota translation: _____

Literal translation: Cat gray eight chickens two (they) chase.

English translation: _____

101. Dakota translation: Wičasta yamŋi ta´ĥca ota kuwapi.

Literal translation: _____

English translation: _____

102. Dakota translation: _____

Literal translation: _____

English translation: The four women ask for seventy-four chairs.

Woonspe Napcinwanka: First-syllable Verbs

THINGS TO LEARN IN THIS LESSON:

- First-syllable verb conjugation

- New verbs

First-syllable Verb Conjugation

In this lesson, we will build on our knowledge of verbs. Remember, to form verbs in Dakota, you must add to the *root verb*. The root verb is usually listed in the dictionary in the third-person singular (S/He/It) form.

In Lesson Six, you learned the subjective pronouns *wa, ya, un, un_pi, ya_pi,* and *pi* and the placement of these pronouns. Here is the new part: with some verbs, the subjective pronouns are placed *after the first syllable* instead of as prefixes, as in Lesson Six. Review the familiar verb *cin* and its conjugation. Then look at the verb *ȟta´ni* (S/He/It works). The only difference is the placement of the subjective pronoun.

The verbs on the following pages all follow this first syllable conjugation scheme.

CIN (S/HE/IT WANTS)			
		You and I want.	**Uncin**
I want.	**Wacin**	We want.	**Uncinpi**
You want.	**Yacin**	You all want.	**Yacinpi**
S/He/It wants.	**Cin**	They want.	**Cinpi**

ȞTANI (S/HE/IT WORKS)			
		You and I work.	**Ȟtaunni**
I work.	**Ȟtawani**	We work.	**Ȟtaunnipi**
You work.	**Ȟtayani**	You all work.	**Ȟtayanipi**
S/He/It works.	**Ȟtani**	They work.	**Ȟtanipi**

FIRST-SYLLABLE VERB CONJUGATION			
		You and I	____**un**____
I	____**wa**____	We	____**un**____**pi**
You	____**ya**____	You all	____**ya**____**pi**
S/He/It	_____	They	____**pi**

New First-syllable Verbs

(The "I" form is provided to enhance your understanding.)

Baksa	S/He/It cuts off (something)	bawaksa
Capa	S/He/It stabs, pierces, punctures (something)	cawapa
E´hde	S/He/It places, puts, sets (something)	ewahde
Ma´ni	S/He/It walks	mawani
Naĥuŋ	S/He/It hears (something)	nawaĥuŋ
Naŝduta	S/He/It slips (with the foot)	nawaŝduta
Piye	S/He/It fixes (something)	piwaye
Tokŝu	S/He/It transports (something)	towakŝu
Waci	S/He/It dances	wawaci
Wo´hdaka	S/He/It chats, converses, talks	wowahdake
Wo´żu	S/He/It plants, sows	wowazu

EXERCISES FOR WOONSPE NAPCIŊWAŊKA

Translate the following:

1. S/He/It chats.

2. S/He/It walks.

3. S/He/It fixes something.

4. S/He/It works.

5. Ehde.

6. Piye.

7. Wohdaka.

8. Naĥuŋ.

Write out the following sentences in the three-line format (Dakota translation, literal translation, and English translation).

9. English: I walk the dog.

10. Dakota: Bdo ota bayaksa.

11. English: We slip with the foot.

12. Dakota: Miniĥoha eyahnake Mazaska ota iyacupi.

13. English: You and I work.

14. English: I fix the two chairs.

15. Dakota: Wacipi.

Translate the following sentences from English to Dakota.

16. The black dog walks.

17. Winona and Caske talk.

18. He plants the brown potato.

19. The man places the food.

20. We dance.

21. You and I hear the brown bear.

22. They hear the water.

23. The four cats walk.

24. The two horses transport the food.

25. You all talk.

26. You walk.

27. I put down the three books.

Translate the following sentences from Dakota to English.

28. Caŋakaŋyaŋkipi watoto tokŝupi.

29. Uŋci naŝduta.

30. Mayanipi.

31. Iyeciŋkaiyopte duta piyaye.

32. Ina aŋpaohotaŋna capa.

33. Anpaohotoŋna ŝakpe wacipi.

34. Bdo wikcemna wouŋźu.

35. Wicaŝta woyute baksa.

36. Ate wowapi ehde.

37. Mato ġi ŝakowiŋ manipi.

38. Taĥca nauŋĥuŋpi.

39. Ciŋkŝi wata piye.

Woonspe Wikcemna: Adjectives

THINGS TO LEARN IN THIS LESSON:

- Review of adjective rules

- New nouns

- New adjectives

Adjective Rules

An adjective is a word that describes "What kind?" "How many?" or "Which one?" We will begin with adjectives that modify a noun. (If an adjective modifies a verb, it becomes an adverb—we will learn these later.) The Dakota adjective words do not change to reflect person or number, and the Dakota nouns do not change to reflect number either. These rules mean you will have to pay attention to the whole sentence to understand it properly.

You have already been introduced to adjectives that describe color and number. We will learn more useful Dakota adjectives in this lesson.

Remember this rule: *Adjectives follow the word they describe.* This rule applies to both the subject and the direct object. If more than one adjective is used, the adjectives follow the noun in the *inverse* order they would in English.

The adjective **ni´na** is placed directly in front of the word you are describing. For example: "Very good day" will become "Aŋpetu nina waśte."

New Nouns

Odowaŋ	song
Zitkaŋa/da	bird
Hituŋkadaŋ	mouse
Aġuyapi	bread

Lots of New Adjectives!

*Te´ca	new/young
Mibe	round or circular
Ohodapica	adorable
Waihakta	affectionate
*Ohitika	tough or furious
*Caŋze	angry or furious
Owaŋyag waśte	beautiful or handsome
Owaŋyag śica	ugly
*Haŋ´ska	tall
*Pte´cedaŋ	short
*Ce´pa	fat
*Tamaheca	skinny

Wi´ži´ca	wealthy
*Waȟpanica	poor
*Uŋŝika	pitiful/in need
Waciŋhnuni	absent-minded
Witkotka	crazy
Witko	foolish
Suta	hard
Paŋpaŋna	soft
Ta´ku ecoŋ	busy
*Ŝi´ca	bad
*Waŝte	good
Wowiȟa	funny
*Ŝa´pesni	clean
*Ŝa´pe	dirty
Ka´ta	hot
Osni	cold
Taŋ´ka	large
Ci´stiŋna	small
Ku´ža	lazy
*Caŋtewaŝte	happy
*Caŋteŝica	sad
Watuka	tired
*Wi´pi	full of food
*Taŋ´yan	sell/good
*Wa´pi	lucky
*Waŝteda	cute
Waditake	brave

*These adjectives will be used in Woonspe Ake Topa.

EXAMPLE SENTENCES

Dakota translation:	Iŋmu caŋtewaŝte hituŋkadaŋ ni´na ġi topa kuwa.
Literal translation:	Cat happy mouse very brown four (it) chases.
English translation:	The happy cat chases the four very brown mice.
Dakota translation:	Wicaŝta haŋska tamaheca wowapi waŝte wowiȟa ciŋ.
Literal translation:	Man tall skinny book good funny (he) wants.
English translation:	The skinny, tall man wants a funny, good book.

Write out the following sentences in the three-line format (Dakota translation, literal translation, and English translation).

1. Wicaṡta ṡuŋkawakaŋ sapa owaŋyag waṡte ciŋ.

2. Hokṡina woyute waṡte ciŋ.

3. The ugly man stabs a hot potato.

4. You and I hear a small chicken.

5. The tired child leaves for home.

6. The poor man fixes the clean chair.

7. The affectionate child takes an adorable dog.

8. The tall man stabs the five clean fish.

9. The cute mouse wants the bread.

10. Find six pictures in a book or on the Internet. Write three different Dakota sentences at least four words long for each picture. Be creative and use your imagination! Use verbs, colors, numbers, other adjectives, and nouns to make your sentences clear. Write sentences in the three-line format (Dakota translation, literal translation, and English translation).

Sentence 1:

Sentence 2:

Sentence 3:

Sentence 4:

Sentence 5:

Sentence 6:

Sentence 7:

Sentence 8:

Sentence 9:

Sentence 10:

Sentence 11:

Sentence 12:

Sentence 13:

Sentence 14:

Sentence 15:

Sentence 16:

Sentence 17:

Sentence 18:

Woonspe Ake Waŋżi: Storytelling

THINGS TO LEARN IN THIS LESSON:

- Importance of storytelling

- Introduction to common Dakota entities

- Dakota creation account

Storytelling

Storytelling (**Ohuŋkaŋkaŋ**) exists as a crucial component to Dakota life. The Dakota language in the past was completely oral—the alphabet we use today was developed from European systems and the language has been adapted for writing. In the past the oral language provided the central means of communication. Through stories, the previous generation passed values, concepts, and proper behavior to the next generation.

- Accounts in story form provide the relevant past to apply to the present situations of life.
- Stories show how to be a good relative and how to understand kinships in order to build good relationships.
- Stories teach the basic values and concepts of living a good life. For example, a story tells how the overall well-being of the **tioŝpaye,** or extended family, overrides individual traits.

Customs, considerations, thoughts, and appropriate behavior dictate the concepts of proper relationships. The way a Dakota person views life becomes an extended family, community, tribal, and national worldview. The unspoken rule is that each individual is part of the whole. Stories teach unity, coexistence, and one's relationships with the world.

Specially gifted people amongst each family and extended family voluntarily and naturally used oral storytelling to teach the tribe's young people. These stories were told in Dakota, and the nuances and richness of the language provided a cultural frame of references that tied the present to the past.

The custom used to be that stories were only told in the winter months and only at nighttime. If a person told stories during the day, especially in the summer, snakes would bring ill fortune and possibly death. Since times have changed, Dakota elders now believe stories can be told anytime.

Many Dakota stories have morals and are told so that the good wins and the bad loses. A main character in many stories is Uŋktomi, the spider or trickster. Uŋktomi is always ready to cheat, steal, and take advantage of others. Uŋktomi rarely wins in the end, and this example serves to teach people that good prevails.

Spiritual Entities

The following are a few of the more important spiritual entities that the Dakota tell stories about. These spirits have their own purpose in many stories, including the Dakota creation story. Throughout the book, we will examine a few of these stories, so keep these important spirits in mind.

Iŋ´yaŋ: Male spirit. The first creative and powerful spirit from whom all things are created. His spirit was **Wakaŋtaŋka.**

Haŋhe´pi: Female spirit. In the beginning of creation, she exists as nothing, the black of darkness. When Haŋhepi marries Wi, she becomes **Haŋwi.** She absorbs some of Wi's light, becoming the most beautiful of spirits.

Maka´: Female spirit. The first to be created from the blood of Iŋyaŋ. She is the mother of all living things and the earth itself.

Maȟpi´yato: Male spirit. The sky and the source of all wisdom and power. He is the great judge, and his decisions are binding upon all others.

Wi: Male spirit. *Wi* is the shortened form of **Aŋpawi** or **Aŋpetuwi.** Wi is the sun, and his light is a source of energy and strength. Wi was originally married to Haŋwi, the moon.

Tate´: Male spirit. Tate, the wind, was a companion to Maȟpiyato. He governed the fourth time, the year. Tate married Ite, and his children were the Four Winds and little Yum.

Uŋktomi: Male spirit. The player of jokes upon humans and animals.

Woope: Female spirit. The Beautiful One, she brought pleasure and harmony to the home. Woope was the daughter of Maȟpiyato and served as the mediator between the spirits and mankind, who call her the White Buffalo Woman. She became the wife of Okaġa.

Dakota Creation

The oral Dakota creation account occurs at the place where the headwaters of the Minnesota and the Mississippi rivers have their origins. This place is called *Bdotemnisota,* Mille Lacs, which is considered to be the middle of all things and the center of the earth. The ancestor of all Dakota people is considered to be **Ishnaicaġe,** a spiritual essence. A number of spiritual beings appear in this story, and these beings also appear throughout the rest of the book and have bearing on the Dakota way of life. In this very long story, we will begin by introducing the first spirits and how they came into existence. We will then continue through the rest of the creation story by introducing new spirits as vocabulary and then learning how they came into existence.

· · ·

Long, long ago, before time, before the existence of anything, there was Iŋyaŋ and Haŋhepi. Haŋhepi, while she was there, she was only the black of darkness. Iŋyaŋ was soft and shapeless, but all the powers of creation existed within his blue blood. Iŋyaŋ desired that there be others, so that he might rule them. He knew that there could be no others unless he created them from himself. He also knew that if he created, he would have to give up part of his spirit and a portion of his blood. The power of the new creation would depend on how much spirit and blood was given up by Iŋyaŋ.

MAKA

Finally, Iŋyaŋ decided to create another, but only as an extension of himself, so he could still control the powers. He took part of himself and spread it over and around himself in the shape of a great disk. He named this disk Maka. In the making of Maka, Iŋyaŋ's veins opened and all of his blood flowed from him. Iŋyaŋ shrank and became hard and powerless.

MAĤPIYATO

As Iŋyaŋ's blood flowed, it became water. Since the powers cannot live in water, they separated and became a great blue dome above Maka. The edges of the dome were at the edges of Maka. This blue dome is now called the sky and is the spirit of Maĥpiyato. Iŋyaŋ, Maka, and the waters have become the world, and Maĥpiyato is the sky above where the powers dwell.

THE DEMANDS OF MAKA

In time, Maka became quarrelsome and scolded Iŋyaŋ. Maka was upset that Iŋyaŋ had not thought to create her as a spirit separate from him. She also demanded that Iŋyaŋ banish the lovely Haŋhepi. Iŋyaŋ, having become powerless after creating Maka and Maĥpiyato, could not do as she wished. Maka insulted Iŋyaŋ for his lack of power and nagged him until he agreed to appeal to Maĥpiyato. To satisfy Maka, Maĥpiyato heard the complaint and the plea of Iŋyaŋ, and in this manner became the final and supreme judge of all things.

Maĥpiyato decreed that Maka must remain forever attached to Iŋyaŋ, just as she was created. To satisfy her, he created Aŋpetu, who is not a spirit but only the red of light. Maĥpiyato banished Haŋhepi to the regions under the world and placed Aŋpetu on the world. Now, there was light everywhere on the world, but there was no heat or shadows.

Maka looked at herself and saw she was naked and cold. Again, she complained to Maĥpiyato about this. Maĥpiyato took something from Iŋyaŋ, from Maka, from the waters, and from himself. From these things, he made a shining disk. Maĥpiyato called this disk *Wi*. Maĥpiyato then placed Wi above the blue dome and commanded him to shine on the entire world, giving heat to everything, and to make a shadow for each thing. Wi did as he was commanded, and all the world became hot.

Now, Maka had no comfort except in the shadow. She implored Maĥpiyato to return Haŋhepi to the world. Patiently, Maĥpiyato commanded **Aŋpetu,** day, and Haŋhepi, night, to follow each other, so that each remained only a short time on the world. He commanded Wi to go to the regions under the world and to follow Aŋpetu and Haŋhepi on the world. Aŋpetu, Haŋhepi, and Wi did as they were told. Haŋhepi became the companion of Wi and showed a soft light which gave light to the darkness. Haŋhepi became known as Haŋwi, the most beautiful of spirits.

The Pte People

In the regions under the world, the spirits had their feasts. There, Maĥpiyato had created mankind, whom he named **Pte People,** to be the servants of the spirits, and they grew the special foods that the spirits like to eat. Mankind increased and became many.

The father and mother of the Pte People were Ate and Huŋ. The people selected a chief named Wazi, whose wife was Wakaŋka. Some of the Pte People came to the surface of the earth and became the ancestors of the Dakota people.

The Four Directions

The story of the four directions began long, long ago, when Wazi lived under the earth with Wakaŋka. They had a daughter, Ite, who grew up to be the most beautiful of all women. Even though Ite was not a spirit, a spirit called Tate fell in love with her. Tate married her and Ite gave birth to quadruplet sons. These four children later became the Four Winds and set the four directions.

UŊKTOMI

After the marriage, Wazi gained prestige because his daughter, Ite, was married to a spirit. Wazi was not satisfied with this honor, though, and desired to have the powers of a spirit. Uŋktomi, the great trickster, knew this and agreed to help Wazi gain this power, if Wazi would help him make others look ridiculous. So it was agreed that Wazi, Wakaŋka, and Ite would assist Uŋktomi. Uŋktomi would then give special powers to Wazi and Wakaŋka and make Ite more beautiful than even the spirit Haŋwi.

WI AND ITE

As Ite became more and more beautiful, she was less and less devoted to Tate and their four sons. Eventually, Wi saw Ite and was deeply struck by her beauty. Wi forgot about his wife, Haŋwi, and invited Ite to the feast of the gods. Through the planning of Uŋktomi, Ite ended up sitting in Haŋwi's place, next to Wi. When Haŋwi arrived, she saw another in her seat of honor. Haŋwi was so ashamed that she hid her face from the laughing people, especially from Uŋktomi, who was laughing the loudest.

MAĤPIYATO'S JUDGMENT

After the feast of the gods, Maĥpiyato called a council and questioned Wi, Ite, Wakaŋka, Wazi, and Uŋktomi. Maĥpiyato then passed the following judgment: Wi and Haŋwi were to be separated. Wi would rule the daytime, and Haŋwi would rule the nighttime. Ite would give premature birth to her last son, and all of her children would be taken from her to live with their father, Tate. Banished to earth, Ite would live there without any friends. She would become **Anoġ-Ite** and have two faces—one of them very beautiful and the other very ugly and horrible. She would be the cause of fighting, temptations, and gossip. Her parents, Wazi and Wakaŋka, were to be banished to the edge of the earth. Uŋktomi was banished to the edge of the earth as well and was to forever remain friendless. Tate was instructed to raise his children properly and do women's work. His sons would grow up and travel over the world, establishing the four directions and undergoing many hardships. Tate's four sons were collectively known as **Tatuyetopa**. They were given the role as messengers between the spirits and mankind.

WOOPE

One day, a beautiful young woman named Woope came to Tate's tipi. She lived with him and his sons and was like a daughter to Tate. She did all the woman's work for Tate. After the four directions were set, the brothers began to court Woope. She desired only Okaġa, and a great feast was given by Tate for the new couple.

Uŋktomi and Anoġ-Ite Trick Mankind

Uŋktomi grew tired of playing pranks upon the animals that roamed the world and sought out Anoġ-Ite. Anoġ-Ite longed to live among her own people again. Together Uŋktomi and Anoġ-Ite thought of a trick to get mankind of the Pte People to come above upon the earth. They knew that if mankind ever tasted meat and learned about tipis, they would want them and surely would come onto the earth.

Anoġ-Ite prepared some food and clothing. She then had a wolf take the food and clothing down to a cave leading to the underworld where mankind lived. The wolf gave the clothing and food to **Tokahe**, the First One.

Soon, Tokahe set out with three other men to find where such good things came from. Uŋktomi and Anoġ-Ite made themselves appear very young and attractive and told the men that they were really very old. Uŋktomi and Anoġ-Ite credited the food of the earth for keeping them young looking. When the men went back to the underworld and told of the wondrous things they had seen and found, many people did not believe them.

However, six men and their families returned with Tokahe to the earth. When they became tired, hungry, and thirsty, Anoġ-Ite tried to comfort them, but they saw the horrible side of her face and were very frightened. Uŋktomi laughed and made fun of them. Tokahe was very ashamed. Wazi and Wakaŋka appeared and led them to the land of the pines. They showed the men how to hunt, how to make clothing and tipis, and how to live well upon the earth. They were the first people on the earth, and their descendents are the Dakota people. Many years passed after Tokahe had led the first men through the cave to the earth.

Many more years passed after the Dakota had become accustomed to living on this earth when a spirit visited them. She came as the White Buffalo Woman to tell mankind of their human powers and to make them more aware of the relationship between man and the spirits.

EXERCISES FOR WOONSPE AKE WAŊŻI

1. How does the Dakota creation account compare to the creation story you are most familiar with? How is it similar? How is it different?

2. The White Buffalo Woman is an important figure in Dakota tradition. Research her role in teaching mankind. How were men to behave? How were they to communicate with the spirits?

3. Create a visual representation of at least six of the main entities within the Dakota creation account. It could be something as simple as a family tree or a drawing of these spirits and their roles in relationship to the world as we understand it today (the sun, the sky, etc.).

Woonspe Ake Noŋpa: Second-syllable Verbs

Second-syllable Verbs

Remember in order to form verbs in Dakota you must add to the root verb. The root verb is usually listed in the dictionary in the third-person singular (S/He/It) form.

You learned the subjective pronouns *wa, ya, un, un_pi, ya_pi,* and *pi* and the placement of these pronouns. You also learned how to place these subjective pronouns after the first syllable in Lesson Eight. Now we will learn the next group of verbs. With this group, the subjective pronouns are placed *after the second syllable.* There isn't a way to recognize which verbs follow each pattern: you must simply memorize each group of verbs.

Review the following verb box, and notice the difference between these verbs and the verbs previously introduced.

Second-syllable Verb Conjugation

OPETUŊ (S/HE/IT BUYS)			
		You and I buy.	**Opeuŋtuŋ**
I buy.	**Opewatuŋ**	We buy.	**Opeuŋtuŋpi**
You buy.	**Opeyatuŋ**	You all buy.	**Opeyatuŋpi**
S/He/It buys.	**Opetuŋ**	They buy.	**Opetuŋpi**

New Second-syllable Verbs

(The "I" form is provided to enhance your understanding.)

Anaġoptaŋ	S/He/It listens	anawaġoptaŋ
Caŋtekiya	S/He/It loves (someone)	caŋtewakiya
Ehaŋki	S/He/It returns to her/his/its origins	ehaŋwaki
Iboto	S/He/It bumps into, collides with (someone or something)	ibowatu
Inaĥni	S/He/It is in a hurry	inawaĥni
Iwohdake	S/He/It talks about, gossips	iwowahdake
Mas´akipa	S/He/It telephones (someone)	masawakipa
Wicada	S/He/It believes (something or someone)	wicawada
Wo´petuŋ	S/He/It shops	wopewatuŋ
Wo´tehda	S/He/It is hungry	wotewahda

Translate the following sentences.

1. They don't buy.

2. You and I listen.

3. I love.

4. We telephone.

5. You believe.

6. They bump into.

7. She doesn't listen.

8. We don't buy.

9. He returns to his origins.

10. You and I are in a hurry.

11. They shop.

12. You talk about (someone).

13. I telephone.

14. You all love.

15. We shop.

16. I return to my origins.

17. They are not in a hurry.

18. You all don't collide with.

19. He is hungry.

20. We love.

21. They gossip.

22. I am hungry.

23. You all don't gossip.

24. We believe.

25. They are hungry.

26. Masakipa.

27. Wicayada.

28. Caŋteyakiyapi.

29. Opwatuŋ.

30. Ehaŋkipi.

31. Iboyatopi.

32. Anaġoptaŋ śni.

33. Wopetuŋpi.

34. Iwouŋhdake.

35. Wopewatuŋ śni.

36. Ehaŋuŋkipi.

37. Caŋtewakiye.

38. Ibotopi.

39. Wotehda.

40. Inayahinipi.

41. Masakipapi.

42. Ibowatu śni.

43. Wicauŋdapi.

44. Inahni.

45. Iwoyahdake.

Woonspe Ake Yamni: "Uŋk" Verbs

**THINGS TO LEARN
IN THIS LESSON:**

- Recognizing when to change the "un" pronoun to "uŋk"
- New verbs
- New nouns

When the addition of *uŋ* precedes a vowel, in both the dual number conjugation (you and I form) and the first-person plural conjugation (we form), the *uŋ* changes to *uŋk*. Review the following three verbs and their conjugated form to become familiar with this conjugation type.

ADI (S/HE/IT STEPS ON [SOMETHING])			
		You and I step on ___.	**Uŋkadi**
I step on ___.	**Awadi**	We step on ___.	**Uŋkadipi**
You step on ___.	**Ayadi**	You all step on ___.	**Ayadipi**
S/He/It steps on __.	**Adi**	They step on ___.	**Adipi**

OWA (S/HE/IT WRITES)			
		You and I write.	**Uŋkowa**
I write.	**Owawa**	We write.	**Uŋkowapi**
You write.	**Oyawa**	You all write.	**Oyawapi**
S/He/It writes.	**Owa**	They write.	**Owapi**

AHI (S/HE/IT BRINGS [SOMETHING])			
		You and I bring ___.	**Uŋkahi**
I bring ___.	**Awahi**	We bring ___.	**Uŋkahipi**
You bring ___.	**Ayahi**	You all bring ___.	**Ayahipi**
S/He/It brings ___.	**Ahi**	They bring ___.	**Ahipi**

New Verbs

The following is a list of new "uŋk" verbs to learn. The "I" and "You and I" forms are provided to enhance your understanding.

		I	"YOU AND I"
Ai	S/He/It arrives there (with something)	Awai	Uŋkai
Akaŝtaŋ	S/He/It pours on to	Awakaŝtaŋ	Uŋkakaŝtaŋ
Aki	S/He/It arrive home there (with something)	Awaki	Uŋkaki
I	S/He/It arrives	Wai	Uŋki
Icu	S/He/It takes or receives (something)	Iwacu	Uŋkicu

Ihuŋni	S/He/It finishes, ends, or concludes/arrives at	Iwahuŋni	Uŋkihuŋni
O	S/He/It shoots and hits (something)	Wao	Uŋko
Ode	S/He/It looks for (something)	Owade	Uŋkode
Ohnaka	S/He/It puts (something) inside	Owahnaka	Uŋkohnaka
Okada	It lays eggs, or S/He scatters, spreads	Owakada	Uŋkokada
Okaŝtaŋ	S/He/It pours	Owakaŝtaŋ	Uŋkokaŝtaŋ
Okihi	S/He/It is able to accomplish	Owakihi	Uŋkokihi
Okiwa	S/He/It writes his own	Owakiwa	Uŋkokiwa
U	S/He/It comes	Wau	Uŋku
Uŋ	S/He/It is	Wauŋ	Uŋkuŋ

New Nouns

Wi´tka	egg
Su	seed or grain
Asaŋ´pi	milk
Haŋpi	juice
Caŋpa´	chokecherry
Caŋo´hnaka	trunk or box
Wo´żuha	empty bag or sack
Wo´żuhadaŋ	small bag
Owe´	footprint, track, or trail
Hoĥpi´	nest

EXERCISES FOR WOONSPE AKE YAMNI

Translate the following sentences:

1. We arrive here with something.

2. You and I put something inside.

3. You pour out.

4. We arrive there with something.

5. You and I look for something.

6. We shoot something.

7. You and I arrive.

8. We finish.

9. We are.

10. You and I write.

11. He is able to.

12. I look for.

13. You all write.

14. She brings juice.

15. We look for a footprint.

16. The bird takes seed.

17. Makawamduŝkadaŋ awadi.

18. Tokiya yati he?

19. Owade asaŋpi.

20. Caŋpa yaciŋpi.

21. Uŋkai.

22. Ŝuŋka nompa hoġan yamni aipi.

23. Cataŋ ḳa Winona haŋpi akipi.

24. Su uŋkokada.

25. Asaŋpi uŋkokaŝtan.

26. Siceca zaptaŋ ŝkatapi.

27. Woyute waciŋ.

28. Ina caŋohnaka taŋka icu.

29. Ate su ota woẑu.

30. Wicasta owe kuwa.

31. Caŋakaŋyaŋkapi ŝakpe uŋkode.

32. Caże owakiwa.

33. Wai.

34. Woẑuhadaŋ owahnaka.

Match the following Dakota word with the correct English word.

35. Aŋpaohotoŋna   a. some

36. Su   b. daughter

37. Witka   c. chokecherry

38. Ŝunkawakaŋ   d. brave

39. Hoĥpi   e. horse

40. Wahaŋpi   f. chicken

41. Bdo   g. black

42. Caŋpa   h. potato

43. Cuŋkŝi   i. soup

44. Oŋġe   j. nest

45. Sapa   k. egg

46. Waditake   l. seed or grain

THINGS TO LEARN
IN THIS LESSON:

- Subjective pronouns

- Personal pronouns

- Distinguishing
  words

- Asking words

- The verb *yuhe/a*

Woonspe Ake Topa: Miscellanea

Pronoun Usage

In English, the verb "to be" is used with predicate adjectives or predicate nominatives (adjectives or nouns) to describe or name the subject. For example, "John is tall. He is a teacher."

These "to be" verbs are "understood" in Dakota because they are incorporated into the predicate adjective—that is, the pronouns are found within the adjective that describes the noun. In these one-word sentences, both the subject and the verb are "understood." These "understood" words will appear in parentheses in literal translations in this book. For example, let's take the adjective *wašte*.

WAŠTE WITH SUBJECTIVE PRONOUNS			
		You and I (are) good.	**Uŋwašte**
I (am) good.	**Mawašte**	We (are) good.	**Uŋwaštepi**
You (are) good.	**Niwašte**	You all (are) good.	**Niwaštepi**
S/He/It (is) good.	**Wašte**	They (are) good.	**Waštepi**

Similarly, the verb for "to be" is not used as an auxiliary verb. (Auxiliary verbs are used in conjunction with a subjective noun and another verb.) Sentences using descriptive words and a noun are written as follows—again the "to be" is understood:

Dakota sentence: Caske haŋska.
Literal translation: Caske (is) tall.
English translation: Caske is tall.

Dakota sentence: Nidakota.
Literal translation: You (are) Dakota.
English translation: You are Dakota.

SUBJECTIVE "TO BE" PRONOUN PATTERN			
		You and I (are).	**Uŋ____**
I (am).	**Ma____**	We (are).	**Uŋ____pi**
You (are).	**Ni____**	You all (are).	**Ni____pi**
S/He/It (is).	**____**	They (are).	**____pi**

Not *all* adjectives can be used in this way! The adjectives marked with an asterisk (*) in Woonspe Wikcemna can be. We will review them here. The "I" form is provided to enhance your understanding.

Te´ca	new/young	mateca
Ohitika	tough/furious	omahitika
Caŋze	angry or furious	caŋmaze
Haŋ´ska	tall	mahaŋska
Pte´cedaŋ	short	maptecedaŋ
Ce´pa	fat	macepa
Tamaheca	skinny	matamaheca
Waĥpanica	poor	mawahpanica
Uŋŝika	pitiful/in need	uŋmaŝika
Wizica	wealthy	wimazica
Ŝi´ca	bad	maŝica
Waŝte	good	mawaŝte
Ŝa´pesni	clean	maŝapeŝni
Ŝa´pe	dirty	maŝape
Caŋtewaŝte	happy	cantemawaŝte
Caŋteŝica	sad	cantemaŝica
Wi´pi	full of food	wimapi
Taŋ´yan	well/good	mataŋyan
Wapi	lucky	wamapi
Waŝteda	cute	mawaŝteda

Remember the title of this lesson—"Miscellanea"? This part of the lesson includes words that are useful but don't constitute enough to have their own chapter. This section is a catch-all.

Other Useful Pronouns

Miye	I
Niye	you
Iye	s/he
Uŋkiye	you and I
Uŋkiyepi	we
Niyepi	you all
Iyepi	they
Mitawa	mine
Nitawa	yours
Uŋkitawa	ours

Distinguishing Words

Hena	those
Dena	these
De	this
Ded	here

For example: Mato hena/Those bear

Asking Words

Tuwe	who
Ta´ku	what
Tohaŋ	when
To´kiya	where
To´keca	why
Tukte	which

Yuhe/a´ (To Have or Possess)

We will end this chapter with *Yuhe/a´*. While this verb conjugates with a different pattern and is the only one of this type that we will introduce at this time, it's an important verb to become familiar with.

Many verbs that end with a/e will follow this pattern. The She/He/It, I, You, and You and I forms will conjugate with the *e* ending, while the We, You all, and They forms will change to the *a* ending.

Notice that Yuhe/a doesn't adhere very well to this pattern either, since there are changes in the way the verb is spelled. Yuhe/a is simply an irregular verb and needs to be memorized.

YUHE/A´ (TO HAVE OR POSSESS)			
		You and I have.	**Uŋyuhe**
I have.	**Bduhe**	We have.	**Uŋyuhapi**
You have.	**Duhe**	You all have.	**Duhapi**
S/He/It has.	**Yuhe**	They have.	**Yuhapi**

Woonspe Ake Zaptaŋ: Woyute (Food)

Food is important to everyday life. Here is a list of easy food-related nouns—some of which you already know!

Note that the word for bread, *aǵuyapi*, is used to make a "family" of bread-related nouns. This example presents a pattern that exists for many words. If the exact phrase, like "fry bread," does not appear in the dictionary, you can simply put together the two words like this: "Aǵuyapi ceǵuǵuyapi."

Waŝtewadake	I like (something).
Wo´tehda	S/He is hungry.
Wo´tewahda	I am hungry.
Ahi	S/He brings (something).
Woyute	food
Aǵuyapi	bread
Aǵuyapi ceǵuǵuyapi	fry bread
Aǵuyapisaka	cracker
Aǵuyapiskuye	cake
Aǵuyapiskuyeŋa/da	cookie
Asaŋpiihdi	butter
Tado´	meat
Asaŋpipasutapi	cheese
Asanpisuta	cheese
Bdo	potato
Bdokaȟpa	potato chip
Wamnaheza	corn
Psiŋ	rice
Pŝin	onion
Taspaŋ	apple
Wažuŝteca	strawberry
Wahaŋpi	soup
Waȟpe baksaksa yutapi	salad
Mini	water
Mni	water
Mniŝni	soda pop
Kapopapida	soda
Asaŋpi	milk
Haŋpi	juice
Peźihu´tasapa	coffee
Peźutasapa	coffee

Wak´ŝica	plate
I´saŋ	knife
Wi´cape	fork
Tu´kiha	spoon
Wi´yatke	cup

The verbs *wo´te/a* and *yute/a* have different conjugation patterns compared to what you have learned so far: memorize them as a bit irregular.

WO´TE (S/HE/IT EATS)			
		You and I eat.	**Wauŋta**
I eat.	**Wawata**	We eat.	**Wauŋtapi**
You eat.	**Wayata**	You all eat.	**Wayatapi**
S/He/It eats.	**Wota**	They eat.	**Wótapi**

YU´TE/A (S/HE/IT EATS [SOMETHING])			
		You and I eat.	**Uŋyate**
I eat.	**Wáte**	We eat.	**Uŋtapi**
You eat.	**Yáte**	You all eat.	**Yátapi**
S/He/It eats.	**Yute**	They eat.	**Yútapi**

EXERCISES FOR WOONSPE AKE ZAPTAŊ

Translate these foods to Dakota words.

1. Bread

2. Banana bread

3. Wheat bread

4. Cake

5. Cookie

6. Cracker

7. Corn bread

8. Fry bread

9. Rye bread

10. Write five simple "I like" sentences in Dakota. (Remember that the direct object will precede the verb.) For example: *Iŋmu waŝtewadake.*

Translate the following sentences.

11. Yatapi.

12. Pŝin waŝtewadake.

13. Tado yatapi.

14. Uŋyate.

15. Uŋci aǧuyapi ceǧuǧuyapi ahi.

16. Wahaŋpi awai.

17. Aǧuyapiskuyeŋa topa waciŋ.

18. Asaŋpipasutapi ḳa aǧuyapisaka waŝtewadake.

19. Wahaŋpi yakacoco.

20. Wiyatke kaptaŋyaŋ.

21. Woyute waŝte.

22. Wowiȟa wiŋ bdo taŋka yute.

23. Makawamduškadaŋ uŋtapi šŋi.

24. Wakšica owasin eyahde.

25. Wotehdapi!

26. I like chokecherries.

27. You all eat bread and butter.

28. Do you have a clean cup?

29. The three men dig up potatoes.

30. The horse eats all the apples.

31. The skinny girl does not eat.

32. Third-born son brings eight clean forks.

33. The man looks for coffee.

34. I like milk and cookies.

35. We have lots of food.

36. I am hungry.

37. I eat rice and onion soup.

38. I want a knife.

39. You all eat the cake.

40. They bring more forks.

Review Exercises

1. What are the three dialects that comprise the Siouan language system?

2. What is the Oceti Ŝakowiŋ? List the Oceti Ŝakowiŋ. Which are Dakota, Lakota, or Nakota?

3. What are the four basic Dakota values as presented previously in this workbook?

4. Dakota words are generally accented on which syllable?

5. Translate: Wicaŝta

6. Translate: Child

7. Translate: Woman

8. List the birth-order names for both boys and girls.

9. A Dakota family has two girls and four boys. What are the children's names?

10. Accent placement: Ciŋ kŝi

11. Accent placement: Tuŋ kaŋ ŝi

12. Accent placement: A te

13. Accent placement: Wiŋ yaŋ

14. Translate: Tokiya ti he?

15. Translate: Taŋyan wauŋ do/ye?

16. Translate: Wowiĥa Wiŋ emakiyapi ye.

17. Translate: Tukte ed htani he?

18. List five non-number words that express quantity.

19. *Som* is a contraction of what word?

20. List the numbers 1 to 10.

21. What does "ake" mean?

22. Write in Dakota: 58

23. Write in Dakota: 12

24. Write in Dakota: 79

25. Write in Dakota: 30

26. Write in Dakota: 92

27. What does it mean to incorporate the subjective pronoun into the verb form?

Conjugate the following in verb boxes.

28. Ciŋ

29. Opetuŋ

30. Owa

31. Mani

32. Ode

33. Ŝa

34. Caŋtekiya

35. Htani

36. I

37. Ti

38. Masakipa

39. Waci

Translate these sentences:

40. Oyawa wowapi.

41. Suŋkawakaŋ inmusuŋka adi.

42. Wiŋyan peżihutasapa kacoco.

43. Aŋpaohotoŋna owasin woyute waŝte ciŋpi.

44. Caŋakaŋyaŋkapi ŝakpe uŋkode.

45. Wahaŋpi yaciŋpi qa waĥpe baksaksa yutapi he?

46. Tokiya ti he?

47. Siceca zaptaŋ uŋyuhapi.

48. Wazuŝteca uŋda.

49. Mniŝni waciŋ.

50. What are you called?

51. You all dig up potatoes.

52. I drive a car.

53. We earn lots of money.

54. We sow grain.

55. The angry woman does not listen.

56. I buy bread.

57. You all are good.

58. I like cake.

59. We eat corn and butter.

Matching

60. Lesson   a. Wahnawotapi

61. Corn   b. Miniȟoha

62. Mouse   c. Oyate

63. Cup   d. Woonspe

64. Egg   e. Caŋakaŋyaŋkapi

65. Goose   f. Caŋohnaka

66. Chokecherry   g. Wamnaheza

67. Fabric   h. Hoȟpi

68. Tribe   i. Hoġan

69. Box   j. Hituŋkadaŋ

70. Book   k. Witka

71. Chair   l. Maga

72. Fish   m. Caŋpa

73. Nest   n. Wowapi

74. Table   o. Wiyatke

Woonspe Ake Ŝakpe: Dakota Values

THINGS TO LEARN IN THIS LESSON:

- Value system
- Twelve Dakota values

Dakota Value System

The Dakota people have a strong value system or way of living that realizes every-thing in life has a special role. The following list includes "truths" or values that the Dakota acknowledge as special.

Oco´wasiŋ means "all, or the whole." Adding *wo* in front of an adjective or verb creates an abstract noun. For example, *waŝte* becomes *wowaŝte* to speak about "goodness." *(Remember that words beginning with "wo" are pronounced with the accent on the first syllable.)*

Wo´ahope Oco´wasiŋ	All observation
Wo´okaĥniġe Ocowasiŋ	All knowledge
Wo´ksape Ocowasiŋ	All wisdom
Wo´caŋtewaŝte Ocowasiŋ	All benevolence
Wo´wicake Ocowasiŋ	All truth
Wo´waŝtedake Ocowasiŋ	All love
Wo´takuye Ocowasiŋ	All relatives
Wo´iyokihi Ocowasiŋ	All values
Wo´wanaġoptan Ocowasiŋ	All obedience
Wo´ohoda Ocowasiŋ	All respect
Wo´wakinihaŋ Ocowasiŋ	All courtesy
Wo´owotaŋna Ocowasiŋ	All honesty
Wo´wicowaĥba Ocowasiŋ	All humility
Wo´waonŝida Ocowasiŋ	All kindness
Wo´yuonihaŋ Ocowasiŋ	All honor
Wo´wicada Ocowasiŋ	All trust
Wo´wiyuŝkiŋ Ocowasiŋ	All joy
Wo´caŋtohnakapi Ocowasiŋ	All generosity
Wo´waditake Ocowasiŋ	All bravery
Wo´waciŋtaŋka Ocowasiŋ	All patience
Wo´kicaŋpte Ocowasiŋ	All consolation
Wo´okiye Ocowasiŋ	All peace

Wodakota Woope Wikcemna Noŋpa (The Twelve Dakota Values)

There are twelve Dakota values that help guide a person through life.

Ocowasiŋ: Wholeness. All things are interrelated. Everything in the universe is part of a single whole and is connected in some way to everything else. It is only possible to understand something if we understand its connections.

To´keca: Changes. Everything is in a state of constant change. One season falls upon the other. People are born, live, and die. All things change. There are two kinds of change: the coming together of things and the coming apart of things. Both kinds of change are necessary and are always connected to each other.

Siŋtomni: Cycles. Change occurs in cycles or patterns. They are not random or accidental. If we cannot see how a particular change is connected, it usually means our viewpoint is affecting our perception.

Maka wiconi and **Wakaŋ wiconi:** Earth life and Sacred life. These two concepts are complementary and are bound to one another.

Wawicaḳupi: People can acquire new gifts, but one must struggle to do so. This process of developing new personal qualities may be called "true learning."

Wo´ksape topa: Four wisdoms. There are four dimensions of *true learning*. A person learns in a whole and balanced manner when the mental, spiritual, physical, and emotional dimensions are involved in the process.

Wicohaŋ wakaŋ topa: The spiritual dimension of human development has four related capacities:
   a. The capacity to have and to respond to dreams, visions, ideals, spiritual teachings, goals, and theories.
   b. The capacity to accept these as a reflection of our unknown or unrealized potential.
   c. The capacity to accept these ideals using symbols in speech, art, or mathematics.
   d. The capacity to use this symbolic expression toward action directed at making the possible a reality.

Wo´okihi: People must actively participate in the development of one's own potential.

Wico owotaŋna: People must *decide* to develop their own potential and actively travel a life path that realizes one's own potential.

Wo´waŝteohŋa: An active journey of self-development will be aided. Any person who sets out on a journey of self-development will be aided by guides, teachers, and protectors.

Wo´ŝicaoŋa: The only source of failure is a person's own failure or unwillingness to follow the teachings.

EXERCISES FOR WOONSPE AKE ŜAKPE

1. There are twenty-two Dakota truths listed. Determine the adjective or verb that creates the abstract noun for each of these truths. For example, *waŝte* becomes *wowaŝte* to speak about "goodness." Be prepared to discuss your answers in class.

2. In the first five of Wodakota Woope Wikcemna Noŋpa, there is an understanding of "balance," connections, and cycles, which is somewhat contrary to Western, linear thinking. With this in mind, draw a picture or write a short story illustrating one of these concepts. Be creative and imaginative.

3. Compare and contrast the first five ideas of Wodakota Woope Wikcemna Noŋpa to another traditional philosophy. It can be another indigenous philosophy, an Eastern philosophy or religion, or a Western religion.

4. Learning is stressed in the latter seven values. Describe how you are actively participating in your development and how you have decided to realize your own potential.

5. Describe an individual who has influenced your life by being your guide, teacher, or protector on your journey of self-development.

Woonspe Ake Ŝakowiŋ: Animal Families

Animal Families

The orderliness of the Dakota language greatly benefits students who are trying to learn it. This orderliness is evident when learning the animal families. Many of the creatures that belong to the four-leggeds **(Hutopa),** the wingeds **(Ḣupahutoŋ),** and the crawlers also belong to families. Once you learn the root word for each family, learning the specific creatures is a lot easier. Of course there are exceptions, but these are few. Many of the animals in Dakota belong to families—the Ta family, the Ŝuŋka family, the Maġa family, the Zitka family, and the Waŋmdi family.

Hutopa: The Ta Family

Ta is the generic term for all ruminating animals, and *ta* often appears in the words for these animals.

Ta	moose
Tataŋka	buffalo
Tabdo´ka	bull buffalo or male deer
Tawiŋye	cow buffalo, cow elk, or doe deer
Pte	cow buffalo
Tahiŋ´casaŋ	antelope
Ta´hiŋca	deer
Táȟca	deer
Taciŋca	fawn
Tatokaŋa	goat
Ta´hcanskaŋa	sheep
Tasŋaheca	striped squirrel
Ta´hcanowaŋpi	domestic sheep
Upaŋ	elk (common)
Hehaka	bull elk

Hutopa: The Ŝuŋka Family

Ŝuŋka forms the root word for these kinds of doglike animals. Note that there can be more than one word for each animal.

Ŝuŋ´ka	dog
Ŝuŋȟpaŋŋa	puppy or little dog
Ŝuŋȟpanda	puppy or little dog

Ŝúŋ´kawakaŋ	horse
Ŝuŋktaŋka	horse
Ŝuŋġbdoka	stallion
Ŝukciŋcadaŋ	colt
Ŝuŋkonaŝoda	a pacing horse
Ŝuŋġwaŋiyaŋpi	domestic dog or horse
Ŝuŋkatokeca	wolf
Ŝuŋgmanitu	wolf
Ŝuŋciŋca	young wolf
Ŝuŋġidaŋ	fox
Ŝuŋġina	gray fox

Other Animals

Mato	bear
Hituŋkadaŋ	mouse
Siŋteŝda	rat (ŝda—no hair on the tail)
Iŋmu	cat
Iŋmuŝuŋka	cat
Iŋmutaŋka	panther (big cat)
Pte	cow
Ca´pa	beaver (ca— tree; pa—pushes over with the head)
Maŝtiŋca	rabbit
Mi´ca	coyote
Mi´caksica	coyote
Zica´	squirrel
Mna´ža	lion

Ĥupahutoŋ: The Zitka Family

Zitka is the generic term for a bird of any kind. Like *Ta*, *Zitka* functions as the root word for naming many different birds. If you add *ŋa* to the end as in "Zitkaŋa," you create the word for a small bird. Note also the word *zi* for "yellow" is found in this root word.

Zitka´	bird
Zitkaŋa	small bird
Zitkataŋka	big bird
Zitkaŋasapa	blackbird
Zitkaŋaŝa	red bird
Zitkaŋato	bluebird or blue jay
Zitkahdeŝka	spotted bird
Zitka´mdeġa	pelican

Ĥupahutoŋ: The Waŋmdi Family

Wambdi is the generic term for eagle. It is also often spelled *Waŋmdi*.

Waŋmdi	royal or war eagle
Waŋmdi hdeŝka	spotted eagle
Waŋmdi zi	golden eagle
Waŋmdiduta	red eagle
Ĥuya	a young eagle
Aŋukasaŋ	bald eagle (Teton)

Ĥupahutoŋ: The Maġa´ Family

Maġa´ refers to the birds that comprise the fowl or **waĥu´pa koza** animal family. Remember to be careful with the accent! "Maġa" (goose) is accented on the second syllable, *ġa*. If you accent the first syllable, *ma,* the meaning of the word changes from "goose" to "garden or field."

Maġa´	goose
Maġaska	domestic goose
Maġa sapa	Canada geese
Maġataŋka	swan
Maġakŝica	duck
Maġa cincaŋa	goslings or ducklings
Paġoŋta	mallard duck

Other Birds

Tanaġidaŋ	hummingbird
Ŝdo´ŝdodaŋ	meadowlark
Cetaŋ	hawk
Uŋkcekiĥa	magpie
Aŋpaohotoŋna	chicken
Ŝiyo	pheasant
Ŝiŝoka	robin
Zizica	turkey
Cetaŋduta	red-tail hawk (aka "chicken hawk")
Uŋciŝicedaŋ	crow (aka the bad grandmother)
Kaŋġi	raven
Heca	buzzard/vulture

Reptiles and Insects

Hoġaŋ	fish
Zuzuhecedaŋ	snake

Hnaŝka	frog
Ke´ya	turtle
Matuska	crab
Ahde´ŝka	lizard
Ahde´ŝkataŋka	crocodile
Caponka	mosquito
Hona´ǧidaŋ	house fly
Tażuŝka	ant
Tuĥmaǧa	bee
Tuĥmaǧa haŋ´ŝka	wasp
Uŋktomi	spider

Wawoyake Iapi (Verbs)

Now that we have covered a wide variety of animals, let's review some verbs that may be used in conjunction with these animal words. You already know many of them.

Kaĥapa	S/He/It drives (something)
Kuwa	S/He/It follows/chases/hunts
Naĥuŋ	S/He/It hears (something)
Ni	S/He/It has life, is alive
Ti	S/He/It lives (somewhere)
Ŝkaŋ	S/He/It moves about
Ŝkata	S/He/It plays
Tokŝu	S/He/It transports

Four verbs have been conjugated for you to use.

WAŊYA´KE/A (S/HE/IT SEES OR PERCEIVES)			
		You and I see.	Waŋuŋyake
I see.	Waŋbdake	We see.	Waŋuŋyakapi
You see.	Waŋdake	All of you see.	Waŋdakapi
S/He/It sees.	Waŋyake	They see.	Waŋyakapi

.IYE´YA (S/HE/IT FINDS [SOMETHING])			
		You and I find.	Iyeuŋya
I find.	Iyewaya	We find.	Iyeuŋyapi
You find.	Iyeyaya	All of you find.	Iyeyayapi
S/He/It finds.	Iyeya	They find.	Iyeyapi

ĶTE (S/HE/IT KILLS)			
		You and I kill.	Uŋķte
I kill.	Waķte	We kill.	Uŋķtepi
You kill.	Yaķte	All of you kill.	Yaķtepi
S/He/It kills.	Ķte	They kill.	Ķtepi

MANI (S/HE/IT WALKS)			
		You and I walk.	Mauŋi
I walk.	Mawaŋi	We walk.	Mauŋipi
You walk.	Mayani	All of you walk.	Mayaŋipi
S/He/It walks.	Mani	They walk.	Manipi

EXERCISES FOR WOONSPE AKE ŜAKOWIŊ

Translate the following sentences from Dakota to English.

1. Tažuŝka cistiŋna psin yute.

2. Mato Hoġan ķte.

3. Šuŋgmanitu caŋze nina ska maŝtiŋca kuwa.

4. Waŋmdi owaŋyagwaŝte wandake.

5. Paġoŋta topa taŋka manipi.

6. Tataŋka ota iyeuŋya.

7. Zitkahdeŝka noŋpa caŋtewaŝte odowaŋ dowaŋpi.

8. Šuŋka ŝakpe uŋktomi ġi opeuŋpi.

9. Inmu ohodapica waihakta waciŋ.

10. Heca uŋŝika tatokaŋa iyeya.

Translate the following from English to Dakota:

11. The fat, lazy cat doesn't chase the mouse.

12. The black panther kills the fawn.

13. We hear the many happy birds.

14. The small funny puppy plays.

15. The four ugly snakes eat the four small frogs.

16. I want a big beautiful white horse.

17. Three red squirrels gossip.

18. The brown rabbit eats the green salad.

19. The ten Canada geese find clear, cold water.

20. The small ducking follows the big duck.

Woonspe Ake Ŝahdoġaŋ: Animal Tales

THINGS TO LEARN IN THIS LESSON:

- "The Great Race"
- "The Story of Eagle Boy"
- "Uŋktomi and Tataŋka"
- "Uŋktomi and the Ducks"

Let's turn our focus to animals and their relationship to humans. To begin with, we will discuss how animals came to be eaten by humans by examining a story called "The Great Race." We'll also learn more about Uŋktomi through some legends.

The Great Race

When the Creator created the earth and all living things upon it, the people and the animals lived in peace. Neither people nor animals ate flesh. Now it happened in the course of many seasons that the buffalo began to think they were the most powerful beings in the world. They came to believe that they had the right to kill and eat other animals, and people as well. The people cried out, "This isn't fair! We humans and the buffalo were created equal. If one or the other must be more powerful, then it should be us!"

The buffalo said, "Let's settle this. We should have a contest to see whether you eat us or we eat you. How about a race?" The people said, "But in a race, you have an unfair advantage—two legs can't compete with four! Suppose we let the birds race for us. They have wings; you have four legs: that makes it more even." The buffalo agreed and said, "We'll choose our fastest runner, and you choose some birds to race for you."

Then some of the other animals said, "We should have the chance to race, too." "That seems only fair," said the buffalo and the people. All of the living things went to a place near Miniŝota, a chain of small lakes near Spirit Lake, Minnesota. There they lined up for the race.

The buffalo chose a young cow called Running Slim Buffalo Woman. She was the fastest of all animals and had never been beaten in a footrace. To race for them, the humans chose four birds—a hummingbird, a meadowlark, a hawk, and a magpie.

In those early days of the world, birds and animals had no color. Now, for the race, they all painted themselves carefully, each creature according to its own medicine, its own vision. For example, the skunk painted a white stripe on its back, the white-tailed deer painted its tail white, and so forth. As the creatures painted themselves for the great race is how they have looked ever since.

The signal to race was then given, and the crowd of runners began toward a hill which was the halfway point. Running Slim took off in a flash, with all of the buffalo cheering her on. For a while Hummingbird flew along with her, but soon he fell back in exhaustion. Meadowlark then took over. Even so, Running Slim kept far ahead, leading the racers with her thundering hooves. Though the race had gone a great distance, Running Slim was still running as if it had only just begun.

By the time Running Slim reached the halfway point, she and Meadowlark were far ahead of the rest of the racers. At the hill, the umpires were shouting, "Now turn and race back to the starting point!" Meadowlark heard this and thought, "I can't make it that far!" He dropped out of the race, but Hawk was there to take over.

Now Hawk, acknowledged to be the fastest of the birds, suddenly shot ahead of Running Slim. The people shouted for joy—but not for long. Hawk's endurance did not match his swiftness, and the sudden burst of speed exhausted him.

Again, Running Slim took the lead, thundering ahead. With her deep chest, powerful legs, and great lungs, it seemed that she could go on forever at that pace. Then, far in the rear, a little black and white dot could be seen coming up swiftly. This was Magpie, flying hard. Magpie was a slow bird but strong hearted and persevering. The buffalo herd paid no attention to Magpie; they were busy cheering Running Slim. The people looked on in silence.

Some of the racers were running so hard now that blood spurted from their mouths and nostrils. This blood colored the earth beneath, which has remained red along the trail where the race was run.

At last, the finish line was in sight. Though Running Slim was powerful and confident, she was beginning to slow. She could feel herself tiring. The other buffalo were grunting and stomping to encourage her. Magpie was still behind but continued to steadily catch up.

Near the end, Running Slim Buffalo Woman was really tired, but she gathered all of her strength for the last burst. Thundering along, her heart nearly burst with the effort. By then, Magpie was even with her. The two sped up, putting the very last of their strength into the race. They neared the sticks, painted red, that stood in the earth, marking the finish line. It was not until they were a handbreadth away from the finish that Magpie finally shot ahead. The people gave a great shout of happiness, and both racers fell exhausted.

The humans won, and the buffalo lost. Ever since, the people have respected the Magpie, never hunting or eating it. As a result of the race, the people became more powerful than the buffalo and all the other animals. From that time on, people have hunted the buffalo for food.

The Story of Eagle Boy

Long ago, a boy was out walking one day when he found a young eagle that had fallen from its nest. He picked up the eagle and took it home to care for it. He made the eagle a place to stay, and each day he went out and hunted for rabbits and other small game to feed it. His mother asked him why he no longer came to work in the fields and help his family. "I must hunt for this eagle," the boy said. So it went on for a long time, and the eagle grew large and strong as the boy hunted and fed it. Now the eagle was large enough to fly away if it wished, but it stayed with the boy who had cared for it so well. The boy's brothers criticized him for not doing his part to care for the fields, but Eagle Boy did not hear them. He cared only for his bird. Even the boy's father, who was an important man in the village, began to criticize him for not helping. But still, the boy did not listen. So it was that the boy's brothers and his older male relatives came together and decided that they must kill the eagle. They decided they would do so when they returned from the fields the following day.

When Eagle Boy came to his bird's cage, he saw that the bird sat there with his head down. Eagle Boy placed a freshly caught rabbit in the cage, but the eagle did not touch it. "What's wrong, my eagle?" said the boy.

Then the eagle spoke, even though it had never spoken before. "My friend, I cannot eat because I am filled with sorrow," said the eagle.

"Why are you troubled?" said the boy.

"It is because of you," said the eagle. "You have not done your work. Instead, you have spent all of your time caring for me. Now your brothers and your older male relatives have decided to kill me so that you will again return to your duties in the village. I have stayed here all of this time because I love you. But now, I must leave. When the sun rises tomorrow, I will fly away and never come back."

"My eagle," said the boy, "I do not wish to stay here without you. You must take me with you!" "My friend, I cannot take you with me," said the eagle. "You would not be able to find your way through the sky. You would not be able to eat raw food." "My eagle," said the boy, "I cannot live here without you." So he begged the eagle, and at last the great bird agreed.

"If you are certain, then you may come with me. But, you must do as I say. Come to me at dawn, after the people have gone down to their work. Bring food to eat on our long journey across the sky. Put the food in pouches that you can sling over your shoulders. You must also bring two strings of bells and tie them to my feet."

That night the boy filled pouches with bread, dried meat, and fruits. He made up two strings of bells, tying them with strong rawhide. The next morning, after the people had gone down to the fields, he went to the eagle's cage and opened it. The eagle spread its wings wide.

"Now," he said to Eagle Boy, "tie the bells to my feet and climb onto my back. Hold on to the base of my wings."

Eagle Boy climbed on, and the eagle began to fly. They rose higher and higher in slow circles above the town and above the fields. The bells on the eagle's feet jingled. The eagle sang, and the boy sang with him. As they sang, the people in the fields below heard them singing. The people also heard the sounds of the bells Eagle Boy had tied to the eagle's feet. They all looked up.

"They are leaving!" the people said. "They are leaving!" Eagle Boy's parents called up to him to return, but he could not hear them. The eagle and the boy rose higher and higher in the sky until they were only a tiny speck. Soon they were gone from the sight of the people on the ground.

The eagle and the boy flew higher and higher until they came to an opening in the clouds. They passed through and came out into the Sky Land. They landed there on Turquoise Mountain, where the Eagle People lived. Eagle Boy looked around the sky world. Everything was smooth and white and as clean as the clouds.

"Here is my home," the eagle said. He took the boy into the city in the sky, and there were eagles all around them. They looked like people, for they took off their wings and their clothing of feathers when they were in their homes.

The Eagle People made a coat of eagle feathers for the boy and taught him to wear it and to fly. It took him a long time to learn, but soon he was able to circle above the land just like the Eagle People. Eagle Boy was an eagle himself.

"You may fly anywhere," the old eagles told him, "anywhere except to the south. Never fly to the South Land."

All went well for Eagle Boy in his new life. One day, though, as he flew alone, he wondered what it was that was so terrible about the south. His curiosity grew, and he flew further and further toward the south. Lower and lower he flew. Soon he saw a beautiful city below with people dancing around red fires.

"There is nothing to fear here," Eagle Boy said to himself as he flew lower still. Closer and closer he came, drawn by the red fires, until he landed. The people greeted him and drew him into the circle. He danced with them all night, and when he grew tired, he was given a place to sleep. When he woke the next morning and looked around, he saw that the fires were gone. The houses no longer seemed bright and beautiful. All around him there was dust, and in the dust there were bones. He looked for his cloak of eagle feathers, wanting to fly away from this city of the dead, but it was nowhere to be found. Then the bones rose up and came together. There were people made of bones all around him! He rose and began to run, and the people made of bones chased him. Just as they were about to catch him, he saw a badger.

"Grandson," the badger said, "I will save you." Then the badger carried the boy down into his hole, and the bone people could not follow. "You have been foolish," the badger said. "You did not listen to the warnings the eagles gave you. Now that you have been to this land in the south, they will not allow you to live with them anymore."

Then the badger showed Eagle Boy the way back to the city of the eagles. It was a long journey, and when the boy reached the eagle city, he could only stand outside the high white walls. The eagles would not let him enter.

"You have been to the South Land," they said. "You can no longer live with us."

At last, the eagle the boy had raised took pity on him. He brought the boy an old and ragged feather cloak. "With this cloak you may reach the home of your own people," he said. "But you can never return to our place in the sky."

So the boy took the cloak of tattered feathers. His flight back down to his people was a hard one, and he almost fell many times. When he landed on the earth in his village, the eagles flew down and carried off his feathered cloak. From then on, Eagle Boy lived among his people. Though he lifted his eyes and watched whenever eagles soared overhead, he shared in the work in the fields, and his people were glad to have him among them.

Uŋktomi

We have already learned about Uŋktomi in previous lessons. He appears in many stories, including the ones that follow. In many cultures there is a "trickster" character who tries to mislead humans and animals into doing evil or foolish deeds. In Dakota this role is fulfilled by Uŋktomi, the spider and trickster. Here are a couple of Dakota legends regarding Uŋktomi. Uŋktomi is not a human, but he is very wise and able to make things happen almost supernaturally to live as he wishes.

UŊKTOMI AND TATAŊKA

During a time of poverty and famine amongst the people, Uŋktomi was walking along a lake when he met a buffalo who asked Uŋktomi where he was going. Uŋktomi told the buffalo that he was thinking of crossing the lake to help out the poor people any way he could. Uŋktomi said that he was having difficulty crossing the large lake, though.

The buffalo agreed to help Uŋktomi across. The buffalo instructed Uŋktomi to go inside of his buttocks and he would swim across while Uŋktomi was safe. As the buffalo swam and swam, Uŋktomi would peek out from time to time to see how near to the shore they were. At last they arrived at the other shore.

When Uŋktomi saw that he was safe, he went back inside the buffalo and attacked the buffalo's heart. He ripped open the buffalo's heart and killed him. Uŋktomi did this so that the hungry people could eat the buffalo and live a while longer.

UŊKTOMI AND THE DUCKS

When Uŋktomi reached the place where the destitute creatures lived, he discovered that they were the Winged People, or Ĥupahutoŋ. After talking to the Ĥupahutoŋ for a while, Uŋktomi realized that they could not help themselves. So Uŋktomi suggested that they build a large grass hut where Uŋktomi could go in and sing to them. Uŋktomi instructed the Ĥupahutoŋ to dance, with the warning that once the dance began, none of them should open their eyes. Uŋktomi said that they must keep their eyes closed for the entire dance, and if anyone did open their eyes, they would have red eyes forever. Uŋktomi began singing, and the Ĥupahutoŋ began to dance. The words in Uŋktomi's song were "those who open their eyes will have red eyes forever." All of the Ĥupahutoŋ began to dance around the hut in a circle. Very soon, one of the Ĥupahutoŋ got too close to Uŋktomi, and Uŋktomi reached out and killed it by wringing its neck. This went on for quite some time until Uŋktomi grabbed a very large goose and had a very difficult time wringing its neck. The goose squawked a shrill cry and caused a little Hell-diver [a kind of duck] to open its eyes to see what the commotion was all about. The Hell-diver saw that many of the Ȟupahutoŋ had already been killed. The remaining wingeds escaped, and the Hell-diver reminded them that Uŋktomi had come to them offering help. To this day, the little Hell-diver has red eyes. Once again, Uŋktomi, the spider, had performed according to his wisdom for his own personal gain and advantage.

EXERCISES FOR WOONSPE AKE ŜAHDOǴAŊ

1. After reading each of the English translations of the Dakota stories, choose one and write a brief description of the lesson to be learned. Do you know of any other stories that carry this same lesson? Be prepared to discuss your opinion in class.

2. Have you ever been tricked into doing something evil or foolish? Describe your personal experience with Uŋktomi.

3. Think about the story "The Great Race" and the consequences of that race. How should we interpret or evaluate our relationship with animals—especially food animals?

Woonspe Ake Napciŋwaŋka: Men and Women

THINGS TO LEARN IN THIS LESSON:

- Dakota family
- Dakota giveaway
- Dakota code of conduct for men and women
- Dakota child-rearing
- The traditional male role
- The traditional female role

This lesson examines the traditional roles that existed for Dakota men and women. As you read this chapter, think about the benefits this traditional lifestyle would have to the people in the past, present, and future.

Dakota Family

Traditional Dakota men and women have different roles in family life. Historically, the men were the providers, as Dakota society was patrilineal. As you can tell from the language, the foundation of the Dakota culture is the family. The teachings including language provide a basis for dealing with all life. The Dakota family can be symbolized by a wheel with many spokes. The family is the middle hub and there are three major spokes: the first spoke is organization, the second is subsistence, and the third is religion. Many other teachings such as education, language, health, work, play, and leadership represent smaller spokes of the wheel. The outer ring of the wheel is society.

There are three units of the Dakota family: **tiwahe**, **tiohnake**, and **tioŝpaye**. *Tiwahe* describes the immediate family, which includes the husband, wife, children, and grandparents plus all blood relatives. *Tiohnake* describes the immediate household, which includes extended family blood relatives that are far and wide across Dakota settlements, communities, reservations, and geographies. Finally, *tioŝpaye* describes the Dakota extended kinship, including adopted relatives, non-Indians married into the family, offspring, and others who are not actual blood relatives. These three units—tiwahe, tiohnake, and tioŝpaye—comprise the overall kinship system. This kinship system is dictated by birth within a family, and kinship terms are dictated by custom within a given family and cultural group.

The Giveaway

The Dakota giveaway constitutes both an ideology and a way of life. The source of all blessings is Wakaŋtaŋka. Wakaŋtaŋka, the Creator, is the greatest gift-giver and the source of all things on Uŋci Maka. In practice, the giveaway results from an event that has meaning to a traditional-minded person. Examples may be when a person is chosen for an outstanding contribution to the community, when a daughter is chosen as a princess, or when an **akicita** (soldier) returns from war. Through giving, a person becomes highly respected and honored as a provider for the people. The more a person gives, the more honor, respect, and dignity is given to the family. The giveaway reinforces the value of generosity as a way of life.

Dakota Code of Conduct for Men and Women

These are the attitudes and virtues that are learned from early childhood.

Bravery: This virtue requires unflinching bravery in life situations and during war, going beyond the normal feats, and counting coup on the enemy. Life and death struggles do not matter, as doing and accomplishing valor is the norm.

Fortitude: Dakota people show mental and emotional strength in facing adversity, temptation, or death.

Wisdom: Ancestral wisdom coupled with just judgment discerns the proper action to take.

Generosity: The family is structured so that life is a symbol of giving. The wealthier one becomes, the more one gives away. People are expected to give away their best materials and goods—even their life.

Other than these four virtues, two more are expected of women.

Truthfulness: Ceremony and testing require that women tell the truth in all situations.

Childbearing: Since women are the mothers of the **Oyate** (family), they share the life-giving gift with Wakaŋtaŋka. Women must be the providers of the heroes of the Dakota people.

Stages of Development

Traditionally, there are five stages of development. In stages one to three, everything happens around you, and you're the center of attention. In stages four and five, you begin to think about others.

1. *Infancy:* The parents have a ceremony for the infant's arrival. The child is given a name to signify that she or he is born into a nurturing circle. During infancy, one is always carried and the child is always within eyesight of either the mother or other family members. The age of infancy, from birth to age two or three, is known as **hokŝiyopa** for both male and female children.

2. *Childhood:* From ages three to ten years, boys are known as **hokŝidaŋ** and girls are known as **wiciŋcaŋa.** There are two stages within this age. From ages three to five years, children venture outside the home with other similarly aged children. These children are still constantly watched and provided with security, nurturance, and guidance. The second stage begins at age six and continues to age eleven. The young boy is known as **koŝka** and the young girl is known as **wikoŝke.**

3. *Adolescence:* From ages eleven to twenty, the young men are known as **koŝka** and the young women are known as **wikoŝke.** They both begin to learn in the

company of others the same age. These young men and women learn from the elders the skills to understand and live the Dakota values.

4. *Adulthood:* **Wicaŝta** and **Winyaŋ.** From late adolescence to adulthood a person begins determining what he or she can do for family and community based on personal skills. The person's role in the community emerges. Courtship and marriage occur. The following are learned:

    a. One cannot be a leader unless one has successfully been an exemplary follower.

    b. The societies are proving grounds—one is acknowledged based solely on one's performance.

    c. One is given a third name at this stage of life, based on a deed for self, family, and community.

5. *Elders:* **Wicahca** and **Wiŋuhca.** The older man and older woman stage of life occurs from age forty-six to one hundred.

The Traditional Male Role

A boy, six to eleven years old, begins learning from his father(s), uncle(s), and grandfather(s) applied skills such as hunting, sports, and daily "chores" through which one serves another, the common good. At ages twelve through sixteen, the young man prepares extensively for his vision quest, and his family is a co-participant in this event. Thereafter, one acquires direction, new clothes, and a new identity by having been given another name. More responsibilities are added in terms of being a provider. The young man is invited to be a member of one or several societies which stress skills as a hunter, warrior, or comparable type through which he performs for the benefit of family and community. For marriage, the young man gives his fiancée's father many horses and goods, which demonstrates his ability to provide. He also gives his bride twenty-eight buffalo hides for a tipi, which she will own as their home. The conjugal act of marriage is understood to be a sacred act of procreation—a participation with the Creator for a new life. The father participates in preparing for the birth of the child and then places the child as his first priority.

The Traditional Female Role

From early childhood, a girl's mother(s), grandmother(s), and aunt(s) teach her appropriate behavior, values, dress, and work. The values emphasized are modesty, humility, patience, courage, generosity, and honesty. From an early age, she is taught how to nurture and be responsible for herself and her younger siblings. She also learns respect for herself and others. In late childhood, females are taught the skills of cooking, sewing, conduct, etiquette, and hospitality. When adolescence occurs, her family sponsors a four-day womanhood ceremony. For four days, her mother(s), grandmother(s), and aunt(s) devote exclusive full-time instruction to her, a new lodge is constructed for her, and on the fourth day a special ceremony of womanhood is held for her, ushering her from childhood to adulthood.

The young woman knows how to observe the rules of courtship, and upon her marriage she becomes the tripod or three center poles of the tipi. She is the foundation of her home, which she owns as well as all the possessions therein. She is the nurturer of her children and her husband. She is the lifegiver. As a mother, she is the transmitter of **Wo´wakaŋ**—*Wo´wa* means purity, innocence, or holiness, and *kaŋ* means the cord or lifeline of mother to child within the womb. The mother has the power to bring forth into visible reality a new life. Her role as mother involves consistently and always placing the needs of the child as her first priority.

EXERCISES FOR WOONSPE AKE NAPCIŊWAŊKA

1. Do you value generosity as a way of life? List specific examples of how your actions show this. Does this philosophy apply to most people you know? Why or why not?

2. Which of these Dakota virtues do you think is the most important? Write a brief paragraph to justify your opinion.

Woonspe Wikcemna Noŋpa: Kinship

THINGS TO LEARN IN THIS LESSON:

- Male kinship terms

- Female kinship terms

Recall that an earlier lesson covered some of the most basic terms for our closest relatives. We will now expand upon that foundation and learn more words for *mitakuye* (my relatives). The following are first-person words to be used when addressing or referring to relatives. Continuing with the cultural theme of traditional gender roles, note that the words may be different depending on whether it is a male or female speaking. As a sign of endearment, add *na* to some of the names.

Dakota I Familial Terms

Wicaŝta	man
Wiŋyaŋ	woman
Wakanheza	child
Siceca	children
Hokŝina/da	boy
Wiciŋyaŋna	girl
Kuŋ´ŝi	paternal grandmother
Tuŋkaŋŝi	paternal grandfather
Uŋci	maternal grandmother
Uŋ´kaŋ	maternal grandfather
Ate	father
Ina	mother
Ciŋkŝi	son
Cuŋkŝi	daughter

BOYS	BIRTH ORDER	GIRLS
Caske	first-born	Winona
Hepaŋ	second-born	Ha´paŋ
Hepi	third-born	Ha´pstiŋ
Ca´taŋ	fourth-born	Waŋ´ske
Hake	fifth-born	Wihake

Male Kinship Terms

Uŋci	maternal grandmother
Uŋ´kaŋ	maternal grandfather
Kuŋ´ŝi	paternal grandmother
Tuŋkaŋ´ŝi	paternal grandfather

Ina	mother
Ate	father
Taŋ-ka´	older sister
Ciŋye	older brother
Taŋ´kŝi	younger sister
Suŋ´ka or Misuŋ	younger brother
Ate	uncle (father's brother)
Dekŝi	uncle (mother's brother)
Tuŋwiŋ	aunt (father's sister)
Ina	aunt (mother's sister)
Tahaŋ´ŝi	male cousin
Haŋka´ŝi	female cousin
Mitawiŋ	my wife
Ciŋkŝi	son
Cuŋkŝi	daughter
Takoża	grandchild
Ciŋkŝi	nephew (brother's son)
Tuŋŝka	nephew (sister's son)
Cuŋkŝi	niece (brother's daughter)
Tuŋżaŋ	niece (sister's daughter)
Kuŋŝi	mother-in-law
Tuŋkaŋ	father-in-law
Taĥaŋ	brother-in-law
Haŋka	sister-in-law

Female Kinship Terms

Uŋci	maternal grandmother
Uŋ´kaŋ	maternal grandfather
Kuŋ´ŝi	paternal grandmother
Tuŋkaŋ´ŝi	paternal grandfather
Ina	mother
Ate	father
Cunwe	older sister
Tibdo	older brother
Taŋke or Mitaŋ	younger sister
Suŋ´ka or Misuŋ	younger brother
Eŝina	uncle (father's brother)
Ate	uncle (mother's brother)
Tuŋwiŋ	aunt (father's sister)
Ina	aunt (mother's sister)
Iĉe´ŝi	male cousin
Iĉepaŋŝi	female cousin
Mihiŋhna	my husband

Ciŋkŝi	son
Cuŋkŝi	daughter
Takoża	grandchild
Tużaŋ	nephew (brother's son)
Ciŋkŝi	nephew (sister's son)
Tużaŋ	niece (brother's daughter)
Cuŋkŝi	niece (sister's daughter)
Uŋci	mother-in-law
Tuŋkaŋ´ŝi	father-in-law
Ŝiĉe	brother-in-law
Iĉepaŋ	sister-in-law

EXERCISES FOR WOONSPE WIKCEMNA NOŊPA

1. Draw a diagram of the Dakota family as described in the chapter. How does this representation differ from your personal idea of family? How is it similar? You can draw a diagram to explain these differences and similarities.

2. Why do you think there are different terms for men and women?

3. Why are some words the same for different relatives?

Match the following Dakota terms with their English translations.

4. man   a. mihiŋhna

5. my husband   b. ciŋkŝi

6. grandchild   c. ina

7. mother   d. takoźa

8. my wife   e. wicaŝta

9. son   f. mitawiŋ

10. father   g. cuŋkŝi

11. daughter   h. ate

Translate the following sentences. Remember to use the proper kinship term for your gender on the English to Dakota sentences.

12. Ciŋye wowiȟa owanyagwaŝte iwohdaka.

13. Uŋci takuecoŋ topa htanipi.

14. Taŋ-ka ohodapica inmu sapa ciŋ.

15. Ate watuka aġuyapi ceġuġuyapi wate.

16. Ina waihakta cantewaŝte dowaŋ.

17. Cuŋkŝi noŋpa ŝuŋka wikcemna yuhapi.

18. Maternal grandmother mixes up the food.

19. The younger sister writes the letter.

20. The two grandchildren step on the banana.

21. Mother earns money.

22. The son is brave and wise.

Woonspe Wikcemna Noŋpa Som Waŋżi: Taŋcaŋ and Heyake

Now that we have explored differences in family life, social roles, and linguistic rules, let's turn to the practical matter of body parts, clothing styles, and materials. To begin, we must learn the Dakota words for parts of the body. After the body words, we will move on to clothing. The descriptive nature of the Dakota language is again evident in both the body words and the clothing words. Many of the words for today's articles of clothing are made up from a combination of Dakota words. Some of the literal translations will be included.

Taŋcaŋ (Body)

(Literal translations appear in parentheses following the word.)

Pa	head
Ite	face
No´ġe	ear
Iŝta	eye
Iŝtaĥehiŋ (eye and hair)	eyebrow
Iŝtaĥepe	eyelashes
Po´ġe	nostrils
Pasu	nose
Tapuŋ	cheek
Iŝti	lip
Pute	upper lip
Putehiŋ (lip and hair)	mustache
I	mouth
Ceżi	tongue
Hi	tooth
Iku	chin
Cehupa	jaw
Nażute	back of head
Tahu	neck
Hiŋyete	shoulder
Isto	arm
Iŝpa	elbow
Napokaŝke	wrist
Nape	hand

Napsukaza	fingers
Napahuŋka	thumb
Napcoka (middle of hand)	palm
Ŝake	nails
Napakaha	back of hand
Maku	chest
Caŋ´kahu	back
Cuwi	waist
Niġe	paunch or stomach
Tezi	belly
Nisehu	hip
Oŋze	buttocks
Co´wohe	pelvis
Ceca	thigh
Hu	leg
Hupahu	knee
Sicoġaŋ	calf
Iŝkahu	ankle
Siha	foot
Siyete	heel
Sicu	sole
Sipa	toes
Sipahuŋka	big toes
Taŋcaŋ akan (body upon)	upon the body
Uka	skin
Hiŋ	hair
Taŋcaŋ mahed (body inside)	inside the body
We	blood
Kaŋ	veins
Huhu	bones
Conica pŝuŋka	muscle
Nasu	brain
Dote	throat
Dotehbeze	windpipe
Caŋte	heart
Caġu	lungs
Tezi	stomach
Pi	liver
Pakŝiŋ	kidney
Ŝupe	intestines

Heyake (Clothing)

(Literal translations appear in parentheses behind the word.)

Wapaha	cap
Wapaha wapoŝtan	hat
Akaŋuŋpi (wear over)	coat
Nakpiyutake	scarf
Napiŋkpayuġaġa	glove
Napiŋkpaotoza	mitten
O´hde uŋpi	shirt
Wicauŋpi (men wear)	shirt
Wiŋuŋpi (women wear)	shirt
Ohdeġaŋgan (*ġaŋgan*—thin/open)	blouse
Ohde co´za (*coza*—comfortable)	sweater
Sanksaŋ nica	dress
Mahenuŋpi (wear inside)	underwear
Unzeoġi	pants/trousers
Huŋska	sock
Iyahdehuŋska	stocking
Can´haŋpa	shoe
Caŋ´haŋpaziŋca (flimsy shoe)	slipper
Miniĥuhaŋpa (fabric shoe)	moccasin
Caŋ´haŋpacaŝiŋhaŋpa (rubber shoe)	overshoe
Cansihanpa	rubber boots

Related Vocabulary

Miniĥuha	cotton/cloth
Taha	leather
Ta taŋkaha	buffalo leather
Caŝiŋhaŋpa	rubber
Wanaþiŋ	necklace
Ma´zanapĉupe (*maza*—metal)	finger rings
Nakpa oiŋ	earrings
Iŝtamaza (metal eyes)	eyeglasses

KIC´UN (S/HE/IT PUTS ON AND WEARS)			
		You and I wear.	**Unk´cun**
I wear.	**Wec´un**	We wear.	**Unk´icunpi**
You wear.	**Yec´un**	All of you wear.	**Yec´unpi**
S/He/It wears.	**Kic´un**	They wear.	**K´cunpi**

UŊ (S/HE/IT USES OR WEARS)			
		You and I wear.	**Uŋkuŋ**
I wear.	**Muŋ**	We wear.	**Uŋkuŋpi**
You wear.	**Nuŋ**	All of you wear.	**Nuŋpi**
S/He/It wears.	**Uŋ**	They wear.	**Uŋpi**

OPETUŊ (S/HE/IT BUYS [SOMETHING])			
		You and I buy.	**Opeuŋtuŋ**
I buy.	**Opewatuŋ**	We buy.	**Opeuŋtuŋpi**
You buy.	**Opeyatuŋ**	All of you buy.	**Opeyatuŋpi**
S/He/It buys.	**Opetuŋ**	They buy.	**Opetuŋpi**

EXERCISES FOR WOONSPE WIKCEMNA NOŊPA SOM WAŊŻI

Translate the following sentences.

1. The white dog wears the blue sweater.

2. Hokšina caŋhapa unzeoġi sapa kicun.

3. Sanksaŋ nica zito yamni opeuŋtuŋpi.

4. The woman wears the beautiful blouse.

5. Wicašta caŋhaŋpapaziŋca kicun.

6. The child wears the adorable dress.

7. Father wears brown leather shoes.

8. Wowiȟawiŋ mahenuŋpi teca opetuŋ.

9. Kuŋši heyake owaŋyag šica opetuŋ.

10. We use new scarves.

11. Napiŋkpaotoza owaŋyag šica kcunpi.

12. Daughter buys small pants.

13. You and I wear clean clothes.

14. Hepi ohde zi topa opetuŋ.

15. They buy beautiful orange socks.

16. Ina unzeoġi opetuŋ šni.

17. Caske wapaha duta kicun.

18. Akaŋunpi noŋpa taŋka opeyatuŋpi.

19. Winona akaŋunpi šapesŋi kicun.

20. Mother wants beautiful blue fabric.

Find the unrelated word in the following groups and cross it out.

21. ohdeuŋpi
    wicauŋpi
    nakpaoiŋ
    ohdecoza

22. minihuha
    taha
    ta taŋkaha
    sanksaŋnica

23. huŋska
    caŋhaŋpa
    napiŋkpaotoza
    miniȟuhaŋpa

24. wapah
    nakpiyutake
    wapah
    wapoštan
    uŋzeoġi

25. mahenuŋpi
    wanapin
    nakpaoiŋa
    mazanapċupe

26. Bring in five pictures cut from a magazine. Be prepared to discuss and describe the pictures with a classmate. Also be prepared to discuss the pictures your classmates and instructor bring.

27. Describe to a classmate what he or she is wearing—". . . . yecun"—and what you are wearing—". . . . wecun."

Woonspe Wikcemna Noŋpa Som Noŋpa: Pastimes and Hobbies

THINGS TO LEARN IN THIS LESSON:

- Hobbies
- Arts and crafts
- Games and competition

Hobbies and "What I Like"

In this unit, we will explore the different pastimes that people enjoy. New Dakota words will be introduced alongside a glimpse into the culture of the Dakota people: their singing, dancing, games, and competition.

Dena wakuwa waŝte wadaka. These hobbies are what I like.

To explain what people like, we will use the root verb **dake/a** (S/He thinks) with the adjective *waŝte.*

A person can like either things (nouns) or to do something (verbs). Whatever is being liked is placed before the main verb *(daka)* in the sentence. See the verb conjugation box below for more information on *daka.*

To show dislike, *ŝni* is placed at the end of the sentence. To say that someone really likes something, the adverb *nina* is placed at the beginning of the sentence. Remember when writing sentences that adjectives go after the nouns they modify and *ka* means "and."

Here are some examples:

Like
Ŝuŋka waŝte wadaka.
Dog good I think.
I like the dog.

Woyute waŝte dakapi.
Food good they think.
They like the food.

Dislike
Ŝuŋka waŝte wadaka ŝni.
Dog good I think not.
I don't like the dog.

Really like
Nina woyute waŝte dakapi.
Really food good they think.
They really like the food.

Liking Verbs

The verb in the sentence must be conjugated to match the subject (who is doing the liking). If you need to review how to conjugate verbs, go back to earlier lessons. A list of verbs to use in this section follows. Some you are familiar with, but some are new.

DAKE/A (S/HE/IT THINKS)			
		You and I think.	**Uŋdake**
I think.	**Wadake**	We think.	**Uŋdakapi**
You think.	**Yadake**	All of you think.	**Yadakapi**
S/He/It thinks.	**Dake**	They think.	**Dakapi**

WAŜTEDAKA (S/HÈ/IT LIKES [SOMETHING])			
		You and I like.	**Waŝteuŋdake**
I like.	**Waŝtewadake**	We like.	**Waŝteuŋdakapi**
You like.	**Waŝteyadake**	All of you like.	**Waŝteyadakapi**
S/He/It likes.	**Waŝtedake**	They like.	**Waŝtedakapi**

Dakota Arts and Crafts

The Dakota always recognize and honor Wakaŋtaŋka, the Supreme Being. Thus, all Dakota perspective of arts, crafts, designs, and decoration infuses an awareness of the divine presence in all of life and our response to his relationship with us. Dreams, visions, actions, and kinship relationships inspire design and craftworks to the benefit of the individual and the entire Oyate. The form and decoration of each piece moves its owner beyond its earthly purpose and tells a personal story. Another's perspectives may influence the individual Dakota if s/he does not imagine and create from an original dream. If this occurs, the design may have no divine meaning. Dakota products have changed through contact with other cultures, and contemporary times may have caused original meaning and significance to be lost. To learn more or to see images of Dakota crafts and artwork, consult the book *The Mystic Warriors of the Plains* by Thomas E. Mails.

Dakota Games

The Dakota people stayed active by playing games. There are games for children, sports for young men and women, and pastimes for adults. There were seasonal games and contests for either two people or teams. When viewing the list, note that the games have been "renamed" to approximate modern-time games. What do you think the games were called in traditional times? Details are pretty sketchy for some of the games listed here. How do you think they were played? Ask your instructor for more information.

WINTER GAMES

Ice sliding: Sled made of bark, and a wooden top. Stick-together game where boys and girls whipped their tops on the ice and forced them together to see which would out-bump and out-spin the rest.

Sledding: Sleds were made of bowed buffalo ribs and, in very cold weather, sheets of rawhide.

Throwing it in: Players chop five holes in the ice on a lake. Players then form a semicircle and spin their tops at the holes. The object was to get the tops to drop in the holes. If one top went into the center hole, the game was over. Each winner received a top each time he won a game from his opponent. The game would continue until one lost his supply of tops.

Hotana cute: Two straight gooseberry sticks, tipped with a bird's tail feather, were attached together by a carved triangular rib bone, forming tiny winged sleds. With these sleds, men would challenge one another to see who could bounce their top the highest.

SUMMER GAMES

La crosse: A stick ball game played by both men and women.

Darts: Men and boys played this game using bows and arrows.

Bowl and dice: Women played this game with specially marked plum pits or stones to represent the dice. Sticks were used for scoring.

Moccasin: Men played this game using four moccasins and a bead.

EXERCISES FOR WOONSPE WIKCEMNA NOŊPA SOM NOŊPA

Translate the following:

1. I like to walk.

2. You like to eat.

3. They like to chase buffalo.

4. You and I like to wear overshoes.

5. He likes to buy rice.

6. Wauŋcipi waŝteuŋdakapi.

7. Ŝuŋkawakaŋ ĥota waŝteuŋdakapi.

8. Aġuyapi ceġuġuyapi waŝtedake.

9. Peźihutasapa waŝteyadakapi.

10. Odowaŋ waŝtewadake.

**THINGS TO LEARN
IN THIS LESSON:**

- Major elements of powwow

- Types of dancers

- Grand Entry

- Wacipi words

Woonspe Wikcemna Noŋpa Som Yamni: Wacipi

Dakota people have held powwows for many generations. Originally a spring gathering to celebrate the seasonal renewal of life, a wacipi is a social and cultural event where individuals can express themselves artistically through song and dance, celebrate their cultural identity, and acknowledge their spirituality while spending time with friends and family. Other ceremonies traditionally conducted during wacipis include naming ceremonies, honoring ceremonies, and ceremonies for dropped eagle feathers.

Major Elements

The major elements of the powwow are drumming, song, dance, and dress. Drum groups provide the music. The drum represents the heartbeat of Mother Earth and the people. Drums are made from wood, hide, or other materials and are considered sacred. The drum is regarded as possessing its own powerful spirit. The drummers form a circle and strike the drum in unison with covered mallets. Each type of song and dance requires a specific style and pace. The songs are about many things: happiness, thanksgiving, nature, war, or mourning. Historically powwow songs were shared between tribes that did not speak the same language; for this reason the words were replaced with chanting so that all groups could join in the singing.

Types of Dancers

There are six types of dancers, and each one wears specific regalia. They enter the arena in the following order.

Men's traditional dancers wear more subdued colors than the other dancers with one bustle of eagle feathers on their back to represent cycles and unity. The regalia usually are decorated with bead- or quillwork. Traditionally these dances were used to tell a story of a great battle or hunt. These dancers often carry items to symbolize their status as warriors such as honor staffs, weapons, or shields. Dances are patterned after animals and birds and as an imitation of tracking or hunting.

Grass dancers have colored ribbons or yarn hanging from their regalia that sway like grass as they dance. Traditionally their entire body moves since the four winds move all of the grasses.

Men's fancy dancers wear colorful regalia with bright feather bustles on their backs and they may wear bells on their legs. As a newer category, this dance is more freestyle, with spins, jumps, and varied body movements. The key is to keep up with the music, showing enthusiasm and energy, and to stop with both feet on the ground when the music stops.

Women's traditional dancers often wear elaborate buckskin or cloth dresses trimmed with quill- or beadwork. Most carry a shawl, and some carry a fan of eagle or hawk feathers. They wear knee-high leggings, which may also be beaded. In this dance, the dancer remains stationary, slightly bobbing up and down in time with the music. The feather fans may be raised at certain points in a song as a sign of pride and honor.

Fancy shawl dancers wear a knee-length cloth dress, beaded moccasins with matching leggings, jewelry, and a fancy shawl. The dancer twirls and spins with fast-paced footwork. This dance was incorporated into the wacipis in the 1970s.

Jingle dress dancers wear a cloth dress embellished with hundreds of metal cones or jingles that make a happy sound as the dancer moves. This dress originated among the Mille Lacs Ojibwe of northern Minnesota but can now be seen at powwows across the country. Dancers keep their feet close to the ground during this dance and step in time with the music.

Decorations on the regalia often have special meaning that express the dancers' feelings, family, or spiritual quest. Regalia are also often adorned with honorings from elders and family.

The Circle

A revered symbol by the Dakota is the circle. Powwows are arranged in concentric circles. The dancers are at the center. The drummers encircle the dancers. The audience forms another circle around the drummers and dancers. Finally, the concessions and vendors may form another circle around the previous three.

The Grand Entry

The powwow begins with the Grand Entry, which is a parade of all the dancers to open the event. *During the Grand Entry, spectators show respect by standing, removing all hats and caps, and abstaining from photography.*

Because akicita or warriors are traditionally honored at powwows, veteran honor guard members lead the procession, first with the eagle staff followed by the flags representing the United States, Canada, the state, and the attending tribes. Following the flags are pageant titleholders like Miss Sisseton Wahpeton Oyate or Miss Indian America, then dignitaries and honored guests.

The dancers enter next, beginning with the males in the order of traditional dancers, grass dancers, and fancy dancers. Women follow, beginning with traditional dancers, fancy shawl dancers, and jingle dress dancers. Teen boys and girls enter next in the same order by regalia types. Finally, small children join the arena.

Until all have entered the arena, the dancers continue dancing clockwise (or sunwise) within the circle. At the end of Grand Entry, often there is a flag song honoring the American flag, a victory song honoring the akicita and all the oyate and people, and then a blessing. The eagle staff is positioned above the U.S. flag signifying First Nation and tied in the center of the arena or stationed at the announcers stand. Once the flag is in place, Grand Entry is over and the powwow dancing and competition begins.

Today's Powwows

Powwow is used interchangeably with *wacipi* because **wacipi** (they dance) is the Dakota-specific word. *Powwow* is believed to have originated from the Algonquin language and now constitutes a term for a meeting or council in general amongst American Indians and non-Indians alike.

Powwows are still a large part of American Indian culture across the United States. The "powwow season" lasts from June to September, with some occurring as early as March. Some American Indian families travel the powwow circuit, attending events across the country. Every weekend they travel to a new location to sing, dance, and celebrate with new and old friends.

Wacipi Words

We will now review some words you learned in previous lessons and add new words to enhance your learning.

Note that some words used as nouns are actually verbs. For example, *wacipi* is the "They" form of the root verb *waci*, which we already know. What other words can you identify as possibly being verbs based on how the word is structured?

Wacipi	dance or powwow
Okawiŋġapi	Grand Entry
Caŋ´ ceġa	drum
Odowaŋ	song
Wicaĥcana wacipi	Men's Traditional Dance
Wiŋyan ahana wacipi	Women's Traditional Dance
Ŝina uŋpi ŝkehaŋ wacipi	Fancy Shawl Dance
Waboga uŋ´pi ŝke´haŋ wacipi	Men's Fancy Dance
Peżi wacipi	Grass Dance
Akicita	warrior or veteran
Makoce noŋpa umanipi	walking in two worlds
Wicohaŋ oŋ wowicakupi	giveaway (given away into the crowd)
Wakaŋheża	children
Witkosŋi	sober

Woonspe Wikcemna Noŋpa Som Topa: Dakota Influence

THINGS TO LEARN IN THIS LESSON:

- Analyzing modern names for Dakota influence

As you know, the Dakota/Lakota/Nakota Nation roamed a vast territory encompassing much of what today are the states of Minnesota, North Dakota, South Dakota, and others. Because the Dakota/Lakota/Nakota were the first people of this area, they named the places in their territory.

European settlers renamed many places, sometimes with a translation of the original name, such as Pipestone or Little Falls. Often they named a place after a saint or their homeland. One only has to look at a map of Minnesota to notice these names, places such as St. Paul, St. Benedict, St. Charles, New London, New Germany, or New Munich.

However, the fact remains that many places have names given to them by the original inhabitants. Perhaps the spelling has changed or the pronunciation is different, but one cannot deny the influence of the Dakota/Lakota/Nakota language in this area's geography.

In addition to the obvious North and South Dakota, *Minnesota* is also a Dakota name, *mini* (water) and *sota* (clear or white). There are the towns of *Wahpeton* (the people dwelling among the leaves) and *Sisseton* (the people of the fish villages), and many others.

Minneota	to drown, or a lot of water
Minneiska	white/clean water
Minnetonka	big water
Chokio	the middle (*Cokaya* was the original name)
Winona	first-born daughter
Chaska	first-born son
Hanska	tall
Taopi	the wound
Hokah	the badger
Waukon	the skin of a bear
Witoka	the female captive
Shakopee	derived from *šakpe*

1. Form a group of two or three. Each member should choose a state—South Dakota, North Dakota, or Minnesota—and search the names within his or her state. What city or place names are derived from Dakota words? What was the original meaning of that word? Which group in the class can find the most?

2. Look to the entire United States. Are there other state names that are American Indian (not just Dakota) names or words? What about cities? What are those state or city names and from which American Indian tribe or nation did they originate?

3. Where else can you find American Indian (not just Dakota) names or themes? Hint: look to different industries—Automobiles? Clothing? Sports? The military?

4. Do you think the average person notices names derived from American Indian sources? Did you know that *Shakopee* was a Native-derived name?

5. What do you think this means? Consider the policies of the past. Have American Indians become assimilated? To what degree, if any?

FINAL NOTE:

Thank you for taking this journey of learning the Dakota language. Our Dakota ancestors paid in land, resources, blood, and tears to allow their children a future. We honor them in many ways but also by protecting our sovereignty, continuing our education, and working for the benefit of our communities and our people. We are strong; we are still here; and we will never fade from the memory of this nation.

Nicolette Knudson

Appendix

Treaty with the Sioux—Sisseton Wahpeton Bands, 1867

Whereas it is understood that a portion of the Sissiton and Warpeton bands of Santee Sioux Indians, numbering from twelve hundred to fifteen hundred persons, not only preserved their obligations to the Government of the United States, during and since the outbreak of the Medewakantons and other bands of Sioux in 1862, but freely perilled their lives during that outbreak to rescue the residents on the Sioux reservation, and to obtain possession of white women and children made captives by the hostile bands; and that another portion of said Sissiton and Warpeton bands, numbering from one thousand to twelve hundred persons, who did not participate in the massacre of the whites in 1862, fearing the indiscriminate vengeance of the whites, fled to the great prairies of the Northwest, where they still remain; and

Whereas Congress, in confiscating the Sioux annuities and reservations, made no provision for the support of these, the friendly portion of the Sissiton and Warpeton bands, and it is believed [that] they have been suffered to remain homeless wanderers, frequently subject to intense sufferings from want of subsistence and clothing to protect them from the rigors of a high northern latitude, although at all times prompt in rendering service when called upon to repel hostile raids and to punish depredations committed by hostile Indians upon the persons and property of the whites; and

Whereas the several subdivisions of the friendly Sissitons and Warpeton bands ask, through their representatives, that their adherence to their former obligations of friendship to the Government and people of the United States be recognized, and that provision be made to enable them to return to an agricultural life and be relieved from a dependence upon the chase for a precarious subsistence: Therefore,

A treaty has been made and entered into, at Washington City, District of Columbia, this nineteenth day of February, A. D. 1867, by and between Lewis V. Bogy, Commissioner of Indian Affairs, and William H. Watson, commissioners, on the part of the United States, and the undersigned chiefs and head-men of the Sissiton and Warpeton bands of Dakota or Sioux Indians, as follows, to wit:

ARTICLE 1.

The Sissiton and Warpeton bands of Dakota Sioux Indians, represented in council, will continue their friendly relations with the Government and people of the United States, and bind themselves individually and collectively to use their influence to the extent of their ability to prevent other bands of Dakota or other adjacent tribes from making hostile demonstrations against the Government or people of the United States.

ARTICLE 2.

The said bands hereby cede to the United States the right to construct wagon-roads, railroads, mail stations, telegraph lines, and such other public improvements as the interest of the Government may require, over and across the lands claimed by said bands, (including their reservation as hereinafter designated) over any route or routes that that may be selected by the authority of the Government, said lands so claimed being bounded on the south and east by the treaty-line of 1851, and the Red River of the North to the mouth of Goose River; on the north by the Goose River and a line running from the source thereof by the most westerly point of Devil's Lake to the Chief's Bluff at the head of James River, and on the west by the James River to the mouth of Mocasin River, and thence to Kampeska Lake.

ARTICLE 3.

For and in consideration of the cession above mentioned, and in consideration of the faithful and important services said to have been rendered by the friendly bands of Sissitons and Warpetons Sioux here represented, and also in consideration of the confiscation of all their annuities, reservations, and improvements, it is agreed that there shall be set apart for the members of said bands who have heretofore surrendered to the authorities of the Government, and were not sent to the Crow Creek reservation, and for the members of said bands who were released from prison in 1866, the following-described lands as a permanent reservation, viz: Beginning at the head of Lake Travers[e], and thence along the treaty-line of the treaty of 1851 to Kampeska Lake; thence in a direct line to Reipan or the northeast point of the Coteau des Prairie[s], and thence passing north of Skunk Lake, on the most direct line to the foot of Lake Traverse, and thence along the treaty-line of 1851 to the place of beginning.

ARTICLE 4.

It is further agreed that a reservation be set apart for all other members of said bands who were not sent to the Crow Creek reservation, and also for the Cut-Head bands of Yanktonais Sioux, a reservation bounded as follows, viz: Beginning at the most easterly point of Devil's Lake; thence along the waters of said lake to the most westerly point of the same; thence on a direct line to the nearest point on the Cheyenne River; thence down said river to a point opposite the lower end of Aspen Island, and thence on a direct line to the place of beginning.

ARTICLE 5.

The said reservations shall be apportioned in tracts of (160) one hundred and sixty acres to each head of a family or single person over the age of (21) twenty-one years, belonging to said bands and entitled to locate thereon, who may desire to locate permanently and cultivate the soil as a means of subsistence: each (160) one hundred and sixty acres so allotted to be made to conform to the legal subdivisions of the Government surveys when such surveys shall have been made; and every person to whom lands may be allotted under the provisions of this article, who shall occupy and cultivate a portion thereof for five consecutive years shall thereafter be entitled to receive a patent for the same so soon as he shall have fifty acres of said tract fenced, ploughed, and in crop: Provided, [That] said patent shall not authorize any transfer of said lands, or portions thereof, except to the United States, but said lands and the improvements thereon shall descend to the proper heirs of the persons obtaining a patent.

ARTICLE 6.

And, further, in consideration of the destitution of said bands of Sissiton and Warpeton Sioux, parties hereto, resulting from the confiscation of their annuities and improvements, it is agreed that Congress will, in its own discretion, from time to time make such appropriations as may be deemed requisite to enable said Indians to return to an agricultural life under the system in operation on the Sioux reservation in 1862; including, if thought advisable, the establishment and support of local and manual-labor schools; the employment of agricultural, mechanical, and other teachers; the opening and improvement of individual farms; and generally such objects as Congress in its wisdom shall deem necessary to promote the agricultural improvement and civilization of said bands.

ARTICLE 7.

An agent shall be appointed for said bands, who shall be located at Lake Traverse; and whenever there shall be five hundred (500) persons of said bands permanently located upon the Devil's Lake reservation there shall be an agent or other competent person appointed to superintend at that place the agricultural, educational, and mechanical interests of said bands.

ARTICLE 8.

All expenditures under the provisions of this treaty shall be made for the agricultural improvement and civilization of the members of said bands authorized to locate upon the respective reservations, as hereinbefore specified, in such manner as may be directed by law; but no goods, provisions, groceries, or other articles— except materials for the erection of houses and articles to facilitate the operations of agriculture—shall be issued to Indians or mixed-bloods on either reservation unless it be in payment for labor performed or for produce delivered: Provided, That when persons located on either reservation, by reason of age, sickness, or deformity, are unable to labor, the agent may issue clothing and subsistence to such persons from such supplies as may be provided for said bands.

ARTICLE 9.

The withdrawal of the Indians from all dependence upon the chase as a means of subsistence being necessary to the adoption of civilized habits among them, it is desirable that no encouragement be afforded them to continue their hunting operations as means of support, and, therefore, it is agreed that no person will be authorized to trade for furs or peltries within the limits of the land claimed by said bands, as specified in the second article of this treaty, it being contemplated that the Indians will rely solely upon agricultural and mechanical labor for subsistence, and that the agent will supply the Indians and mixed-bloods on the respective reservations with clothing, provisions, &c., as set forth in article eight, so soon as the same shall be provided for that purpose. And it is further agreed that no person not a member of said bands, parties hereto whether white, mixed-blood, or Indian, except persons in the employ of the Government or located under its authority, shall be permitted to locate upon said lands, either for hunting, trapping, or agricultural purposes.

ARTICLE 10.

The chiefs and head-men located upon either of the reservations set apart for said bands are authorized to adopt such rules, regulations, or laws for the security of life and property, the advancement of civilization, and the agricultural prosperity of the members of said bands upon the respective reservations, and shall have authority, under the direction of the agent, and without expense to the Government, to organize a force sufficient to carry out all such rules, regulations, or laws, and all rules and regulations for the government of said Indians, as may be prescribed by the Interior Department: Provided, That all rules, regulations, or laws adopted or amended by the chiefs and head-men on either reservation shall receive the sanction of the agent.

In testimony whereof, we, the commissioners representing the United States, and the delegates representing the Sissiton and Warpeton bands of Sioux Indians, have hereunto set our hands and seals, at the place and on the day and year above written.

Lewis V. Bogy   W. H. Watson.
Commissioner of Indian Affairs.

Signed in the Presence of —

Charles E. Mix.
Gabriel Renville, head chief Siss(i)ton and Wa(r)peton bands.
Wamdiupiduta, his x mark, head Siss(i)ton chief.
Tacandupahotanka, his x mark, head Wa(r)peton chief.
Oyehduze, his x mark, chief Sissiton.
Umpehtutokca, his x mark, chief Wahpeton.
John Otherday.
Akicitananjin, his x mark, Sissiton soldier.
Waxicunmaza, his x mark, Sissiton soldier.
Wasukiye, his x mark, Sissiton soldier.
Wamdiduta, his x mark, Sissiton soldier.
Hokxidanwaxte, his x mark, Sissiton soldier.
Wakanto, his x mark, Sissiton soldier.
Ecanajinke, his x mark, Sissiton soldier.
Canteiyapa, his x mark, Sissiton soldier.
Tihdonica, his x mark, Sissiton soldier.
Tawapahamaza, his x mark, Sissiton soldier.
Wandiiyeza, his x mark, Sissiton soldier.
Tacunrpipeta, his x mark, Sissiton soldier.
Wicumrpinumpa, his x mark, Wa(r)peton soldier.
Xupehiyu, his x mark, Wa(r)peton soldier.
Ecetukiye, his x mark, Wa(r)peton soldier.
Kangiduta, his x mark, Wa(r)peton soldier.

Witnesses to signatures of above chiefs and soldiers:

Charles E. Mix.
Benj'n Thompson.
J. R. Brown.
Anexus M. A. Brown, Interpreter.
Chas. Crawford.
Thos. E. McGraw.
J. H. Leavenworth.
A. B. Norton.
Geo. B. Jonas.
Frank S. Mix.

English to Dakota Glossary

The page number where each word first appears is in parentheses following the Dakota translation.

Absent-minded, Waciŋhnuni (37)
Adorable, Ohodapica (36)
Adult male, 20–45, Wicaśta (11)
Adult woman, 20–45, Wiŋ´yaŋ (75)
Affectionate, Waihakta (36)
Again, Ake (15)
All, Owasin (16)
All, or the whole, Oco´wasiŋ (59)
All Benevolence, Wo´caŋtewaśte Ocowasiŋ (59)
All Bravery, Wo´waditake Ocowasiŋ (59)
All Consolation, Wo´kicaŋpte Ocowasiŋ (59)
All Courtesy, Wo´wakinihaŋ Ocowasiŋ (59)
All Generosity, Wo´caŋtohnakapi Ocowasiŋ (59)
All Honesty, Wo´owotaŋna Ocowasiŋ (59)
All Honor, Wo´yuonihaŋ Ocowasiŋ (59)
All Humility, Wo´wicowaȟba Ocowasiŋ (59)
All Joy, Wo´wiyuśkiŋ Ocowasiŋ (59)
All Kindness, Wo´waonśida Ocowasiŋ (59)
All Knowledge, Wo´okaȟniǧe Ocowasiŋ (59)
All Love, Wo´waśtedake Ocowasiŋ (59)
All Obedience, Wo´wanaǧoptan Ocowasiŋ (59)
All Observation, Wo´ahope Oco´wasiŋ (59)
All Patience, Wo´waciŋtaŋka Ocowasiŋ (59)
All Peace, Wo´okiye Ocowasiŋ (59)
All Relatives, Wo´takuye Ocowasiŋ (59)
All Respect, Wo´ohoda Ocowasiŋ (59)
All Trust, Wo´wicada Ocowasiŋ (59)
All Truth, Wo´wicake Ocowasiŋ (59)
All Values, Wo´iyokihi Ocowasiŋ (59)
All Wisdom, Wo´ksape Ocowasiŋ (59)
And, Ḳa (27)
And, Q̇a (27)
Angry, Caŋze (36)
Ankle, Iśkahu (81)
Ant, Taẑuśka (65)
Antelope, Tahiŋ´casaŋ (62)
Apple, Taspaŋ (53)

Arm, Isto (80)
Aunt: father's sister, Tuŋwiŋ (78)
Aunt: mother's sister, Ina (78)

Back, Caŋ'kahu (81)
Back of hand, Napakaha (81)
Back of head, Naẑute (80)
Bad, Ŝi´ca (37)
Bald eagle (Teton), Aŋukasaŋ (64)
Bear, Mato (63)
Beautiful, handsome, Owaŋyag waśte (36)
Beaver, Ca´pa (63)
Bee, Tuȟmaǧa (65)
Belly, Tezi (81)
Big bird, Zitkataŋka (63)
Big toes, Sipahuŋka (81)
Bird, Zitkaŋa (63)
Bird (generic), Zitka´ (63)
Black, Sa´pa (16)
Blackbird, Zitkaŋasapa (63)
Blood, We (81)
Blouse, Ohdeǧaŋǧan (82)
Blue, To (16)
Bluebird or blue jay, Zitkaŋato (63)
Boat, Wa´ta (27)
Body, Taŋcaŋ (80)
Bones, Huhu (81)
Book, Wo'wapi (27)
Box, Caŋo´hnaka (48)
Boy, Hokśina/da (11)
Boy, 3–10 years old, Hokśidaŋ (74)
Boy, 6–11 years old, Kośka (74)
Brain, Nasu (81)
Brave, Wadetale (37)
Bread, Aǧuyapi (36)
Brother-in-law (Female usage), Ŝiĉe (79)
Brother-in-law (Male usage), Taȟan (78)

Brown, Ġi (16)
Buffalo, Tataŋka (62)
Buffalo leather, Ta taŋkaha (82)
Bull buffalo or male deer, Tabdo´ka (62)
Bull elk, Hehaka (62)
Busy, Ta´ku econ (37)
But, Tka (27)
Butter, Asaŋpiihdi (53)
Buttocks, Oŋze (81)
Buzzard, Heca (64)

Cake, Aġuyapiskuye (53)
Calf (body part), Sicoġan (81)
Canada goose, Maġa sapa (64)
Cap, Wapaha (82)
Car, I´yeciŋkaiyopte (27)
Cat, Iŋmuŝuŋka (27)
Cat (abbreviated), Iŋmu (27)
Chair, Caŋ´akaŋyaŋkapi (27)
Changes, To´keca (60)
Cheek, Tapuŋ (80)
Cheese, Asaŋpipasutapi, Asanpisuta (53)
Chest, Maku (81)
Chicken, Aŋpaohotoŋna (21)
Chicken hawk, Cetaŋduta (64)
Child, Wakaŋheża (11)
Children, Siceca (11)
Chin, Iku (80)
Chokecherry, Caŋpa´ (48)
Circular, Mibe (36)
Clean, Ŝa´pesni (37)
Cloth moccasin, Miniĥuhaŋpa (82)
Cloth or cotton, Miniĥuha (82)
Clothing, Heyake (82)
Coat, Akaŋuŋpi (82)
Coffee, Peżihu´tasapa (53)
Coffee, Peżu'tasapa (53)
Cold, Osni (37)
Colt, Ŝukciŋcadaŋ (63)
Cookie, Aġuyapiskuyeŋa (53)
Corn, Wamnaheza (53)
Council fire, Oceti (3)
Courageous, Waditale (37)

Cow, Pte (62)
Cow buffalo, Pte (62)
Cow buffalo, Tawiŋye (62)
Cow elk, Tawiŋye (62)
Coyote, Mi´ca (63)
Coyote, Mi´caksica (63)
Crab, Matuska (65)
Cracker, Aġuyapisaka (53)
Crazy, Witkotka (37)
The Creator, Iŋyaŋ (40)
The Creator, Wakaŋtaŋka (4)
Crocodile, Ahde´ŝkataŋka (65)
Crow (aka the bad grandmother), Uŋciŝicedaŋ (64)
Cup, Wi´yatke (54)
Cute, Waŝteda (37)
Cycles, Siŋtomni (60)

Dakota extended kinships, Tioŝpaye (39)
Dakota value, Wicoĥaŋ wakaŋ topa (60)
Dakota value, Wico owotaŋna (60)
Dakota value, Wo´okihi (60)
Dakota value, Wo´ŝicaoŋa (60)
Dakota value, Wo´wasteohŋa (60)
Dakota value, Changes, To´keca (60)
Dakota value, Cycles, Siŋtomni (60)
Dakota value, Earth life, Maka wiconi (60)
Dakota value, Four wisdoms, Wo´ksape topa (60)
Dakota value, Sacred life, Wakaŋ wiconi (60)
Dakota value, True learning, Wawicaḳupi (60)
Dakota value, Wholeness, Oco'wasiŋ (59)
Daughter, Cuŋkŝi (11)
Daughter of Wazi and Wakaŋka, Ite (42)
Day, Aŋpetu (41)
Deer, Ta´hiŋca (27)
Deer (abbreviated), Ta´ĥca (27)
Dirty, Ŝa´pe (37)
Doe deer, Tawiŋye (62)
Dog, Ŝuŋ´ka (27)
Dog or horse, domestic, Ŝuŋġwaŋiyaŋpi (63)
Dress, Sanksaŋ nica (82)
Drum, Caŋ´ ceġa (90)
Duck, Maġakŝica (64)
Dwellers at the End, Ihaŋktoŋwaŋ (4)

Dwellers on the Plains, Ti´toŋwaŋ (4)
Dwelling, Ti´pi (27)

Eagle (alternative spelling), Waŋmdi (64)
Eagle (generic), Wambdi (64)
Ear, No´ġe (80)
Earrings, Nakpa oiŋa (82)
Earth, Maka (26)
Earthworm, Makawamduŝkadaŋ (27)
Egg, Wi´tka (48)
Eight, Ŝahdoġaŋ (15)
Eighteen, Ake ŝahdoġaŋ (15)
Eighty, Wikcemna ŝahdoġaŋ (15)
Elbow, Iŝpa (80)
Elder female, 45+, Wiŋuhca (75)
Elder male, 45+, Wicahca (75)
Eleven, Akewaŋżi (15)
Elk (common), Upaŋ (62)
Empty bag/sack, Wo´żuha (48)
Eye, Iŝta (80)
Eyebrow, Iŝtaĥehiŋ (80)
Eyeglasses, Iŝtamaza (82)
Eyelashes, Iŝtaĥepe (80)

Fabric, Miniĥoha, miniĥuha (27)
Face, Ite (80)
Family, extended, Tiohnake (73)
Family, immediate, Tiwahe (73)
Fancy Shawl Dance, Ŝina uŋpi ŝkehaŋ wacipi (90)
Fat, Ce´pa (36)
Father, Ate (11)
Father-in-law (Female usage), Tuŋkaŋ´ŝi (79)
Father-in-law (Male usage), Tuŋkaŋ (78)
Fawn, Taciŋca (62)
Female cousin (Female usage), Iĉepaŋŝi (78)
Female cousin (Male usage), Haŋka´ŝi (78)
Female spirit, brings pleasure and harmony to a
    home, Wo´ope (40)
Female spirit, the first to be created, Maka´ (40)
Female spirit, marries Wi, becomes Haŋwi,
    Haŋhe´pi (40)
Few, To´nana (16)
Field or garden, Ma´ġa (10)
Fifteen, Ake zaptaŋ (15)

Fifth-born daughter, Wihake (11)
Fifth-born son, Hake (11)
Fifty, Wikcemna zaptaŋ (15)
Fifty-five, Wikcemna zaptaŋ som zaptaŋ (16)
Finger rings, Ma´zanapĉupe (82)
Fingers, Napsukaza (81)
First-born daughter, Winona (11)
First-born son, Caske (11)
The first creative spirit from whom all things are
    created, Iŋ´yaŋ (40)
The First One, Tokahe (43)
Fish, Hoġaŋ (27)
Five, Za´ptaŋ (15)
Fog, Þo (9)
Food, Wo´yute (27)
Foolish, Witko (37)
Foot, Siha (81)
Footprint, Owe´ (48)
Fork, Wi´cape (54)
Forty, Wikcemna topa (15)
Four, To´pa (15)
Four-legged creatures, Hutopa (62)
Four Wisdoms, Wo´ksape topa (60)
Fourteen, Ake topa (15)
Fourth-born daughter, Waŋ´ske (11)
Fourth-born son, Ca´taŋ (11)
The fowl family, Waĥu´pa koza (64)
Fox, Ŝuŋġidaŋ (63)
Frog, Hnaŝka´ (65)
Fry bread, Aġuyapi ceġuġuyapi (53)
Full of food, Wi´pi (37)
Funny, Wo´wiĥa (37)
Furious, Caŋze (36)
Furious, Ohitika (36)

Garden or field, Ma´ġa (10)
Girl, Wiciŋyaŋna (11)
Girl, 3–10 years old, Wiciŋcaŋa (74)
Girl, 6–11 years old, Wikoŝke (74)
Giveaway (given away to the crowd), Wicohaŋ oŋ
    wo´wicakupi (90)
Glove, Napiŋkpayuġaġa (82)
Goat, Tatokaŋa (62)
Golden eagle, Waŋmdi zi (64)

Good, Taŋ'yaŋ (37)
Good, Waŝte (37)
Good Health, Zani waŝte (13)
Goose, domestic, Maġaska (64)
Goose, or generic reference to fowl, Maġa´ (64)
Goslings or ducklings, Maġa cincaŋ (64)
Grain, Su (48)
Grand Entry, Okawiŋġapi (90)
Grandchild, Takoża (78)
Grass Dance, Peżi wacipi (90)
Gray, Ĥo´ta (16)
Gray fox, Ŝuŋġina (63)
Great Spirit, Wakaŋtaŋka (4)
Green, Watoto (16)
Green, Zito (16)

Hair, Hiŋ (81)
Hand, Nape (80)
Handsome, beautiful, Owaŋyag waŝte (36)
Happy, Caŋtewaŝte (37)
Hard, Suta (37)
Hat, Wapaha wapoŝtan (82)
Hawk, Cetaŋ (64)
He, Iye (51)
Head, Pa (9)
Heart, Caŋte (81)
Heel, Siyete (81)
Hello, yes (man), Hau (13)
Hello, yes (woman), Haŋ (13)
Here, Ded (52)
Hip, Nisehu (81)
Hobbies, Wakuwa (85)
Horse, common, Ŝuŋ´kawakaŋ (27)
Horse, common (alternative), Ŝuŋtaŋka (27)
Horse or dog, domestic, Ŝuŋġwaŋiyaŋpi (63)
Hot, Ka´ta (37)
House fly, Hona´ġidaŋ (65)
Hummingbird, Tanaġidaŋ (64)
Hundreds, Opawiŋġe (15)
Husband (My husband), Mihiŋhna (78)

I, Miye (51)
I am hungry, Wo´tewahda (53)
I like (something), Waŝtewadake (53)

The immediate family, Tiwahe (73)
The immediate household, Tiohnake (73)
Infancy, Hokŝiyopa (74)
Inside the body, Taŋcaŋ mahed (81)
Intestines, Ŝupe (81)

Jaw, Cehupa (80)
Juice, Haŋpi (48)

Kidney, Pakŝiŋ (81)
Knee, Hupahu (81)
Knife, I´saŋ (54)

Lamp, Pe´tiżaŋżaŋ (27)
Large, Taŋ´ka (37)
Lays eggs (It), Okada (48)
Lazy, Ku´ża (37)
Leather, Taha (82)
Leg, Hu (81)
Lesson, Wo´onspe (19)
Letter, Wo´wapi (27)
Life, Wiconi (60)
Lifeline from mother to child, Kaŋ (76)
Lifeline of innocence or sacredness, Wo´wakaŋ (76)
Lion, Mna´ża (63)
Lip, Iŝti (80)
Little Dwellers at the End, Ihaŋktoŋwaŋna (4)
Liver, Pi (81)
Lizard, Ahde´ŝka (65)
Lots, O´ta (16)
Lucky, Wa´pi (37)
Lungs, Caġu (81)

Magpie, Uŋkcekiĥa (64)
Male cousin (Female usage), Iĉe´ŝi (78)
Male cousin (Male usage), Tahaŋ´ŝi (78)
Male deer or bull buffalo, Tabdo´ka (62)
Male spirit, Aŋpawi (40)
Male spirit, Aŋpetawi (40)
Male spirit, the first, Iŋ´yaŋ (40)
Male spirit, the judge and source of wisdom and power, Maĥpi´yato (40)
Male spirit, the sun, Aŋpawi or Aŋpetuwi, Wi (40)
Male spirit, the wind, Tate´ (40)

Male spirit, trickster, Uŋktomi (39)
Mallard duck, Paġoŋta (64)
Man, Wicaŝta (11)
Man (abbreviated), Wica (11)
Man's shirt, Wicauŋpi (82)
Many, O´ta (16)
Maternal grandfather, Uŋ´kaŋ (11)
Maternal grandmother, Uŋci (11)
Meadowlark, Ŝdo´ŝdodaŋ (64)
Meat, Tado´ (53)
Men's Fancy Dance, Waboga uŋ´pi ŝke´haŋ wacipi (90)
Men's Traditional Dance, Wicaĥcana wacipi (90)
Milk, Asaŋ´pi (48)
Mine, Mitawa (51)
Mist, Þo (9)
Mitten, Napiŋkpaotoza (82)
Money, Ma´zaska (27)
Moose, Ta (62)
More, Saŋ'pa (16)
More (contraction), Som (16)
Mosquito, Capoŋka (65)
Mother, Ina (11)
Mother-in-law (Female usage), Uŋci (79)
Mother-in-law (Male usage), Kuŋŝi (78)
Mouse, Hituŋkadaŋ (36)
Mouth, I (80)
Muscle, Conica pŝuŋka (81)
Mustache, Putehiŋ (80)

Nails, Ŝake (81)
Neck, Tahu (80)
Necklace, WanaÞiŋ (82)
Negative: not, no, Ŝŋi (28)
Nephew: brother's son (Female usage), Tużaŋ (79)
Nephew: brother's son (Male usage), Ciŋkŝi (78)
Nephew: sister's son (Female usage), Ciŋkŝi (79)
Nephew: sister's son (Male usage), Tuŋŝka (78)
Nest, Hoĥpi´ (48)
New, Te´ca (36)
Niece: brother's daughter (Female usage), Tużaŋ (79)
Niece: brother's daughter (Male usage), Cuŋkŝi (78)
Niece: sister's daughter (Female usage), Cuŋkŝi (79)
Niece: sister's daughter (Male usage), Tużaŋ (78)

Nine, Napciŋwaŋka (15)
Nineteen, Ake napciŋwaŋka (15)
Ninety, Wikcemna napciŋwaŋka (15)
None, Wanica (16)
Nose, Pasu (80)
Nostrils, Po´ġe (80)
Nothing, Ta´kuna ŝni (16)

Older brother (Female usage), Tibdo (78)
Older brother (Male usage), Ciŋye (78)
Older sister (Female usage), Cunwe (78)
Older sister (Male usage), Taŋ-ka´ (78)
Once, Waŋ´ca (16)
One, Waŋ´ca, waŋżi (15)
One hundred, hundreds, Opawiŋġe (15)
Onion, Pŝin (53)
Orange, Ŝazi (16)
Orange, Zi´ġi (16)
Ours, Uŋkitawa (51)
Overshoe, Caŋ´haŋpacaŋŝiŋhaŋpa (82)

Pacing horse, Ŝuŋkonaŝoda (63)
Palm, Napcoka (81)
Panther, Iŋmutaŋka (63)
Pants or trousers, Unzeoġi (82)
Paper, Wo´wapi (27)
Paper (white), Wo´wapiska (27)
Paternal grandfather, Tuŋkaŋ´ŝi (11)
Paternal grandmother, Kuŋ´ŝi (11)
Paunch or stomach, Niġe (81)
Pelican, Zitka´mdeġa (63)
Pelvis, Co´wohe (81)
People Dwelling Among the Leaves, Waĥpetoŋwaŋ (3)
People of the Fish Village, Sisitoŋwaŋ (4)
Pheasant, Ŝiyo (64)
Plate, Wak´ŝica (54)
Pitiful, poor, Uŋŝika (37)
Poor (without money), Waĥpanica (37)
Poor, pitiful, Uŋŝika (37)
Potato, Bdo (27)
Potato chip, Bdokaĥpa (53)
Powwow, "They dance", Wacipi (90)
Puppy or little dog, Ŝuŋĥpanna, suŋĥ´panda (62)

Purity, Wo´wa (76)
Purple, Tostaŋ (16)

Rabbit, Maŝtiŋca (63)
Rat, Siŋteŝda (63)
Raven, Kaŋġi (64)
Red, Du´ta (16)
Red, Ŝa (16)
Red bird, Zitkaŋaŝa (63)
Red eagle, Waŋmdiduta (64)
Red-tail hawk or chicken hawk, Cetaŋduta (64)
Relative (My relative), Mitakuye (11)
Rice, Psiŋ (53)
Robin, Ŝiŝoka (64)
Round, circular, Mibe (36)
Royal or war eagle, Waŋmdi (64)
Rubber, Caŋŝiŋhaŋpa (82)
Rubber boots, Cansihanpa (82)
Ruler of the Pte People, Wazi (42)
Ruminating animals (generic), Ta (62)

Sacred, Wakaŋ (60)
Sad, Caŋteŝica (37)
Salad, Waȟpe baksaksa yutapi (53)
Santee Bands dialect, Dakota (3)
Scarf, Nakpiyutake (82)
Scarlet, Du'ta (9)
Second-born daughter, Ha´paŋ (11)
Second-born son, Hepaŋ (11)
Seed, Su (48)
Servants to the spirits, Pte People (42)
Seven, Ŝakowiŋ (15)
Seventeen, Ake ŝakowiŋ (15)
Seventy, Wikcemna ŝakowiŋ (15)
She, Iye (51)
S/He/It arrives, I (47)
S/He/It arrives home there (with something), Aki (47)
S/He/It arrives there (with something), Ai (47)
S/He/It asks for (something), Da (21)
S/He/It believes (something or someone), Wicada (45)
S/He/It brings (something), Ahi (47)
S/He/It bumps into/collides with (something), Iboto (45)

S/He/It buys (something), Opetuŋ (45)
S/He/It calls (to someone), Kipaŋ (21)
S/He/It chats, converses, talks, Wo´hdaka (34)
S/He/It comes, U (48)
S/He/It cuts (something), Kaksa (21)
S/He/It cuts off (something), Baksa (34)
S/He/It dances, Waci´ (34)
S/He/It digs up (something), Ḱa (21)
S/He/It drives (something), Kaȟapa (21)
S/He/It earns, Kamna (20)
S/He/It eats, Wo´te (54)
S/He/It eats (something), Yu'te (54)
S/He/It finds (something), Iye´ya (65)
S/He/It finishes, ends, or concludes, Ihuŋni (48)
S/He/It fixes/repairs (something), Piye (34)
S/He/It follows, flirts, chases, hunts, pursues, Kuwa (20)
S/He/It gives (something), Ḱu (21)
S/He/It gossips, Iwohdake (45)
S/He/It has life, is alive, Ni (20)
S/He/It has or possesses, Yuhe/a' (52)
S/He/It hears (something), Naȟuŋ (34)
S/He/It is, uses, or wears, Uŋ (48)
S/He/It is able to accomplish, Okihi (48)
S/He/It is alive, has life, Ni (20)
S/He/It is hungry, Wo´tehda (45)
S/He/It is in a hurry, Inaȟni (45)
S/He/It kills, Ḱte (66)
S/He/It leaves/sets out for home, Hde (21)
S/He/It likes (something), Waŝtedake (86)
S/He/It listens, Anaġoptaŋ (45)
S/He/It lives (somewhere), Ti (20)
S/He/It looks for (something), Ode (48)
S/He/It loves (someone), Caŋtekiye (45)
S/He/It moves about, Ŝkaŋ (21)
S/He/It places, puts, sets (something), E´hde (34)
S/He/It plants or sows, Wo´żu (34)
S/He/It plays, Ŝkata (21)
S/He/It pours, Okaŝtaŋ (48)
S/He/It pours on to, Akaŝtaŋ (47)
S/He/It puts (something) inside, Ohnaka (48)
S/He/It returns/comes back, Hdi (21)
S/He/It returns to her/his/its origins, Ehaŋki (45)
S/He/it scatters or spreads, Okada (48)

S/He/It sees or perceives, Waŋya´ke/a (65)

S/He/It shoots and hits (something), O (48)

S/He/It shops, Wopetuŋ (45)

S/He/It shouts or yells, Ŝa (21)

S/He/It shows or points out, Kipazo (21)

S/He/It slips, slides (with the foot), Naŝduta (34)

S/He/It stabs/pierces/punctures (something),
    Capa´ (34)

S/He/It steps on (something), Adi (47)

S/He/It stirs/mixes up (something), Kacoco (21)

S/He/It takes or receives (something), Icu (47)

S/He/It talks about/gossips, Iwohdake (45)

S/He/It telephones (someone), Mas'akipa (45)

S/He/It thinks, Dake/a (85)

S/He/It transports (something), Tokŝu´ (34)

S/He/It turns or flips (with an instrument),
    Kaptaŋyaŋ (21)

S/He/It walks, Ma´ni (34)

S/He/It wants, Ciŋ (20)

S/He/It wears, Kic'uŋ (82)

S/He/It works, Hta´ni (33)

S/He/It writes, Owa (47)

S/He/it writes his own, Okiwa (48)

Sheep, Ta´hcaŋskaŋa (62)

Sheep, domestic, Ta´hcaŋowaŋpi (62)

Shirt, O´hde uŋpi (82)

Shoe, Caŋ´haŋpa (82)

Shooters Among the Leaves People, Wahpekute (3)

Short, Pte´cedaŋ (36)

Shoulder, Hiŋyete (80)

Sister-in-law (Female usage), Icepaŋ (79)

Sister-in-law (Male usage), Haŋka (78)

Six, Ŝa´kpe (15)

Sixteen, Ake ŝakpe (15)

Sixty, Wikcemna ŝakpe (15)

Sixty-one, Wikcemna zaptaŋ som zaptaŋ (16)

Skin, Uka (81)

Skinny, Tamaheca (36)

The Sky, Mahpi'yato (40)

Slipper, Caŋ´haŋpazincâ (82)

Small, Ci´stiŋna (37)

Small bag, Wo´żuhadaŋ (48)

Small bird, Zitkaŋa (36)

Snake, Zuzuhecedaŋ (64)

Sober, Witkosŋi (90)

Sock, Huŋska (82)

Soda pop, Mniŝni, Kapopapida (53)

Soft, Paŋpaŋna (37)

Soldier or warrior, Akicita (73)

Sole, Sicu (81)

Some, Oŋġe (16)

Son, Ciŋkŝi (11)

Song, Odowaŋ (36)

Soup, Wahaŋpi (27)

Spider, Uŋktomi (65)

The Spirit Lake People, Mdewakaŋtoŋwaŋ (3)

Spiritual essence, the ancestor of the Dakota
    people, Ishnaicaġe (40)

Spoon, Tu´kiha (54)

Spotted bird, Zitkahdeŝka (63)

Spotted eagle, Waŋmdi hdeŝka (64)

Squirrel, Zica´ (63)

Stallion, Ŝuŋġbdoka (63)

Stockings, Iyahdehuŋska (82)

Stomach, Tezi (81)

Storytelling, Ohuŋkaŋkaŋ (39)

Strawberry, Ważuŝteca (53)

Striped Squirrel, Tasŋaheca (62)

Swan, Maġataŋka (64)

Sweater, Ohde co´za (82)

The Sun, Wi (40)

Table, Wa´hnawotapi (27)

Tall, Haŋ´ska (36)

Tate's Four Sons, Tatuyetopa (43)

Ten, Wikcemna (15)

Teton Bands dialect, Lakota (3)

Thank you, Pidamaya (13)

These, Dena (52)

They, Iyepi (51)

Thigh, Ceca (81)

Third-born daughter, Ha´pstiŋ (11)

Third-born son, Hepi (11)

Thirteen, Akeyamni (15)

Thirty, Wikcemna yamni (15)

This, De (52)

Those, Hena (52)

Three, Ya´mni (15)

Throat, Dote (81)

Thumb, Napahuŋka (81)

Tired, Watuka (37)

To give you, Ciču (9)

Toes, Sipa (81)

Tongue, Ceži (80)

Tooth, Hi (80)

Tough, Ohitaka (36)

Track, Owe´ (48)

Trail, Owe´ (48)

Tribe, nation, people, band, Oyate (74)

Trickster, Uŋktomi (40)

Trousers or pants, Unzeoġi (82)

True Learning, Wawicaḳupi (60)

Trunk, Caŋo´hnaka (48)

Turkey, Zizica (64)

Turtle, Ke´ya (65)

Twelve, Ake noŋpa (15)

Twenty, Wikcemna noŋpa (15)

Twenty-six, Wikcemna noŋpa som šakpe (16)

Two, Noŋ´pa (15)

Two-faced Woman, previously known as Ite, Anoġ-Ite (43)

Ugly, Owaŋyag šica (76)

Uncle: father's brother (Female usage), Ešina (78)

Uncle: father's brother (Male usage), Ate (78)

Uncle: mother's brother (Female usage), Ate (78)

Uncle: mother's brother (Male usage), Dekši (78)

Underwear, Mahenuŋpi (82)

Upon the body, Taŋcaŋ akan (81)

Upper lip, Pute (80)

Veins, Kaŋ (81)

Very, Ni´na (36)

Vulture, Heca (64)

Waist, Cuwi (81)

Walking in two worlds, Makoce noŋpa umanipi (90)

War eagle, Waŋmdi (64)

Warrior, Akicita (73)

Wasp, Tuȟmaġa haŋ´ška (65)

Water, Mini (27)

Water, Mni (53)

We, Uŋkiyepi (51)

Wealthy, Wi´ži'ca (37)

Well, Ito (27)

Well, Taŋ´yaŋ (13)

What, Taku (52)

Wheat, Su (48)

When, Tohaŋ (52)

Where, To'kiya (52)

Which, Tukte (52)

White, Ska (16)

Who, Tuwe (52)

Why, To'keca (52)

Wife (My wife), Mitawiŋ (78)

Wife to Wazi, Wakaŋ´ka (42)

Windpipe, Dotehbeze (81)

Winged animals, Ȟupahutoŋ (62)

Wisdom, Wo'ksape (59)

Wolf, Šuŋgmanitu (63)

Wolf, Šuŋkatokeca (63)

Woman, Wiŋ´yaŋ (11)

Woman (abbreviated), Wiŋ (11)

Woman's shirt, Wiŋuŋpi (82)

Women's Traditional Dance, Wiŋyan ahana wacipi (90)

Wrist, Napokaške (80)

Yankton Bands dialect, Nakota (3)

Yellow, Zi (16)

Yes or hello (man), Hau (13)

Yes or hello (woman), Haŋ (13)

You, Niye (51)

You all, Niyepi (51)

You and I, Uŋkiye (51)

Young, Te´ca (36)

Young eagle, Ȟuya (64)

Young man, 11–20 years old, Koška (74)

Young wolf, Šuŋciŋca (63)

Young woman, 11–20 years old, Wikoške (74)

Younger brother, Misuŋ (78)

Younger brother, Suŋ´ka (78)

Younger sister (Female usage), Mitaŋ (78)

Younger sister (Female usage), Taŋke´ (78)

Younger sister (Male usage), Taŋ´kši (78)

Yours, Nitawa (51)

Dakota to English Glossary

The page number where each word first appears is in parentheses following the English translation.

Adi, S/He/It steps on (something) (47)

Aġuyapi, Bread (36)

Aġuyapi ceġuġuyapi, Fry bread (53)

Aġuyapisaka, Cracker (53)

Aġuyapiskuye, Cake (53)

Aġuyapiskuyeŋa, Cookie (53)

Ahde´ŝka, Lizard (65)

Ahde´ŝkataŋka, Crocodile (65)

Ahi, S/He brings (something) (47)

Ai, S/He/It arrives there (with something) (47)

Akaŋuŋpi, Coat (82)

Akaŝtaŋ, S/He/It pours on to (47)

Ake, Again (15)

Ake napciŋwaŋka, Nineteen (15)

Ake noŋpa, Twelve (15)

Ake ŝahdoġaŋ, Eighteen (15)

Ake ŝakowiŋ, Seventeen (15)

Ake ŝakpe, Sixteen (15)

Ake topa, Fourteen (15)

Ake waŋźi, Eleven (15)

Ake yamni, Thirteen (15)

Ake zaptaŋ, Fifteen (15)

Aki, S/He/It arrives home there (with something) (47)

Akicita, Soldier or warrior (73)

Anaġoptaŋ, S/He/It listens (45)

Anoġ-Ite, Two-faced Woman, previously known as Ite (43)

Aŋpaohotoŋna, Chicken (21)

Aŋpawi, Male spirit (40)

Aŋpetawi, Male spirit (40)

Aŋpetu, Day (41)

Aŋukasaŋ, Bald eagle (Teton) (64)

Asaŋ´pi, Milk (48)

Asaŋpiihdi, Butter (53)

Asaŋpipasutapi, Cheese (53)

Asaŋpisuta, Cheese (53)

Ate, Father (11)

Ate, Uncle: father's brother (Male usage) (78)

Ate, Uncle: mother's brother (Female usage) (78)

Baksa, S/He/It cuts off (something) (34)

Bdo, Potato (27)

Bdokaĥpa, Potato chip (53)

Caġu, Lungs (81)

Can´haŋpa, Shoe (82)

Cansihanpa, Rubber boots (82)

Caŋ´ceġa, Drum (90)

Caŋ´akaŋyaŋkapi, Chair (27)

Caŋ´haŋpacaŋŝiŋhaŋpa, Overshoe (82)

Caŋ´haŋpaziŋca, Slipper (82)

Caŋ´kahu, Back (81)

Caŋo´hnaka, Trunk or box (48)

Caŋpa´, Chokecherry (48)

Caŋte, Heart (81)

Caŋtekiye, S/He/It loves (someone) (45)

Caŋteŝica, Sad (37)

Caŋtewaŝte, Happy (37)

Caŋze, Furious, angry (36)

Ca´pa, Beaver (63)

Capa´, S/He/It stabs, pierces, or punctures (something) (34)

Capoŋka, Mosquito (65)

Caske, First-born son (11)

Caŝiŋhaŋpa, Rubber (82)

Ca´taŋ, Fourth-born son (11)

Ceca, Thigh (81)

Cehupa, Jaw (80)

Ce´pa, Fat (36)

Cetaŋ, Hawk (64)

Cetaŋduta, Red-tail hawk or chicken hawk (64)

Ceźi, Tongue (80)

Ciċu, To give you (9)

Ciŋ, S/He/It wants (20)

Ciŋkŝi, Nephew: brother's son (Male usage) (78)

Cinkśi, Nephew: sister's son (Female usage) (79)

Cinkśi, Son (11)

Cinye, Older brother (Male usage) (78)

Ci′stinna, Small (37)

Conica pśunka, Muscle (81)

Co′wohe, Pelvis (81)

Cunwe, Older sister (Female usage) (78)

Cunkśi, Daughter (11)

Cunkśi, Niece: brother's daughter (Male usage) (78)

Cunkśi, Niece: sister's daughter (Female usage) (79)

Cuwi, Waist (81)

Da, S/He/It asks for (something) (21)

Dake/a, S/He/It thinks (85)

Dakota, Santee Bands dialect (3)

De, This (52)

Ded, Here (52)

Dekśi, Uncle: mother's brother (Male usage) (78)

Dena, These (52)

Dote, Throat (81)

Dotehbeze, Windpipe (81)

Du′ta, Red, scarlet (16)

Ehanki, S/He/It returns to her/his/its origins (45)

E′hde, S/He/It places, puts, sets (something) (34)

Eśina, Uncle: father's brother (Female usage) (78)

Ġi, Brown (16)

Hake, Fifth-born son (11)

Han, Hello, yes (woman) (9)

Hanhe′pi, Female spirit, marries Wi, becomes Hanwi (40)

Hanka, Sister-in-law (Male usage) (78)

Hanka′śi, Female cousin (Male usage) (78)

Hanpi, Juice (48)

Han′ska, Tall (36)

Hanwi, Female spirit, married to Wi (40)

Ha′pan, Second-born daughter (11)

Ha′pstin, Third-born daughter (11)

Hau, Hello, yes (man) (9)

Hde, S/He/It leaves/sets out for home (21)

Hdi, S/He/It returns/comes back (21)

Heca, Buzzard, vulture (64)

Hehaka, Bull elk (62)

Hena, Those (52)

Hepan, Second-born son (11)

Hepi, Third-born son (11)

Heyake, Clothing (82)

Hi, Tooth (80)

Hin, Hair (81)

Hinyete, Shoulder (80)

Hitunkadan, Mouse (36)

Hnaśka′, Frog (65)

Hoġan, Fish (27)

Hoĥpi′, Nest (48)

Hokśidan, Boy, 3–10 years old (74)

Hokśina/da, Boy (11)

Hokśiyopa, Infancy (74)

Hona′ġidan, House fly (65)

Ĥo′ta, Gray (16)

Hta′ni, S/He/It works (33)

Hu, Leg (81)

Huhu, Bones (81)

Hunska, Sock (82)

Hupahu, Knee (81)

Hutopa, Four-legged creatures (62)

Ĥupahuton, Winged animals (62)

Ĥuya, Young eagle (64)

I, Mouth (80)

I, S/He/It arrives (47)

Iboto, S/He/It bumps into/collides with (something) (45)

Icu, S/He/It takes or receives (something) (47)

Iĉepan, Sister-in-law (Female usage) (79)

Iĉepanśi, Female cousin (Female usage) (78)

Iĉe′śi, Male cousin (Female usage) (78)

Ihanktonwan, Dwellers at the End (4)

Ihanktonwanna, Little Dwellers at the End (4)

Ihunni, S/He/It finishes, ends, or concludes (48)

Iku, Chin (80)

Ina, Aunt: mother's sister (78)

Ina, Mother (11)

Inaĥni, S/He/It is in a hurry (45)

Inmu, Cat (27)

Inmuśunka, Cat (27)

Inmutanka, Panther (63)

Iŋ´yaŋ, The first creative spirit from whom all things are created, The Creator (40)

I´saŋ, Knife (54)

Ishnaicaġe, Spiritual essence, the ancestor of the Dakota people (40)

Isto, Arm (80)

Iŝkahu, Ankle (81)

Iŝpa, Elbow (80)

Iŝta, Eye (80)

Iŝtahehiŋ, Eyebrow (80)

Iŝtahepe, Eyelashes (80)

Iŝtamaza, Eyeglasses (82)

Iŝti, Lip (80)

Ite, Daughter of Wazi and Wakaŋka (42)

Ite, Face (80)

Ito, Well (27)

Iwohdake, S/He/It talks about, gossips (45)

Iyahdehuŋska, Stocking (82)

Iye, She or he (51)

I´yeciŋkaiyopte, Car (27)

Iyepi, They (51)

Iye´ya, S/He/It finds (something) (65)

Ḳa, And (27)

Ḳa, S/He/It digs up (something) (21)

Kacoco, S/He/It stirs/mixes up (something) (21)

Kahapa, S/He/It drives (something) (21)

Kaksa, S/He/It cuts something (21)

Kamna, S/He/It earns (20)

Kaŋ, Veins, lifeline from mother to child (81)

Kaŋġi, Raven (64)

Kapopapida, Soda pop (53)

Kaptaŋyaŋ, S/He/It turns or flips (with an instrument) (21)

Ka´ta, Hot (37)

Ke´ya, Turtle (65)

Kic'un, S/He/It wears (82)

Kipaŋ, S/He/It calls (to someone) (21)

Kipazo, S/He/It shows or points out (21)

Koŝka, Boy, 6–11 years old (74)

Koŝka, Young man, 11–20 years old (74)

Ḳte, S/He/It kills (66)

Ḳu, S/He/It gives (something) (21)

Kuŋ´ŝi, Mother-in-law (Male usage) (78)

Kuŋ´ŝi, Paternal grandmother (Male usage) (77)

Kuŋ´ŝi, Paternal grandmother (11)

Kuwa, S/He/It follows, flirts, chases, hunts, pursues (20)

Ku´ża, Lazy (37)

Lakota, Teton Bands dialect (3)

Ma´ġa, Garden, field (10)

Maġa´, Goose, or generic reference to fowl (64)

Maġa cincaŋa, Goslings or ducklings (64)

Maġakŝica, Duck (64)

Maġa sapa, Canada goose (64)

Maġaska, Goose, domestic (64)

Maġataŋka, Swan (64)

Mahenuŋpi, Underwear (82)

Mahpi´yato, Male spirit, the judge and source of wisdom and power, The Sky (40)

Maka, Earth (26)

Maka´, Female spirit, the first to be created (40)

Maka wiconi, Dakota value, Earth life (60)

Makawamduŝkadaŋ, Earthworm (27)

Makoce noŋpa umanipi, Walking in two worlds (90)

Maku, Chest (81)

Ma´ni, S/He/It walks (34)

Mas'akipa, S/He/It telephones (someone) (45)

Maŝtiŋca, Rabbit (63)

Mato, Bear (63)

Matuska, Crab (65)

Ma´zanapĉupe, Finger rings (82)

Ma´zaska, Money (27)

Mdewakaŋtoŋwaŋ, The Spirit Lake People (3)

Mibe, Round, circular (36)

Mi´ca, Coyote (63)

Mi´caksica, Coyote (63)

Mihiŋhna, Husband (My husband) (78)

Mini, Water (27)

Minihoha, Fabric (27)

Minihuha, Cloth or cotton (82)

Minihuhaŋpa, Cloth moccasin (82)

Misuŋ, Younger brother (78)

Mitakuye, Relative (My relative) (11)

Mitaŋ, Younger sister (Female usage) (78)

Mitawa, Mine (51)

Mitawiŋ, Wife (My wife) (78)
Miye, I (51)
Mna´ża, Lion (63)
Mni, Water (53)
Mniŝni, A soft drink, soda, pop (53)

Naĥuŋ, S/He/It hears (something) (34)
Nakota, Yankton Bands dialect (3)
Nakpa oiŋa, Earrings (82)
Nakpiyutake, Scarf (82)
Napahuŋka, Thumb (81)
Napakaha, Back of hand (81)
Napciŋwaŋka, Nine (15)
Napcoka, Palm (81)
Nape, Hand (80)
Napiŋkpaotoza, Mitten (82)
Napiŋkpayuġaġa, Glove (82)
Napokaŝke, Wrist (80)
Napsukaza, Fingers (81)
Nasu, Brain (81)
Naŝduta, S/He/It slips, slides (with the foot) (34)
Nażute, Back of head (80)
Ni, S/He/It has life, is alive (20)
Niġe, Paunch or stomach (81)
Ni´na, Very (36)
Nisehu, Hip (81)
Nitawa, Yours (51)
Niye, You (51)
Niyepi, You all (51)
No´ġe, Ear (80)
Noŋ´pa, Two (15)

O, S/He/It shoots and hits (something) (48)
Oceti, Council fire (3)
Oco´wasiŋ, Dakota value, All, or the whole (59)
Ode, S/He/It looks for (something) (48)
Odowaŋ, Song (36)
Ohde co´za, Sweater (82)
O´hde uŋpi, Shirt (82)
Ohdeġaŋgan, Blouse (82)
Ohitika, Tough or furious (36)
Ohnaka, S/He/It puts (something) inside (48)
Ohodapica, Adorable (36)
Okada, It lays eggs, or S/He scatters, spreads (48)

Okaŝtaŋ, S/He/It pours out (48)
Okawiŋġapi, Grand Entry (90)
Okihi, S/He/It is able to accomplish (48)
Okiwa, S/He/It writes his own (48)
Oŋġe, Some (16)
Oŋze, Buttocks (81)
Opawiŋġe, One hundred, hundreds (15)
Opetuŋ, S/He/It buys (something) (45)
Osni, Cold (37)
O´ta, Lots, many, a lot (16)
Owa, S/He/It writes (47)
Owaŋyag ŝica, Ugly (36)
Owaŋyag waŝte, Beautiful, handsome (36)
Owasin, All (16)
Owe´, Footprint, track, or trail (48)
Oyate, A people, tribe, nation, or band (74)

Pa, Head (9)
Paġoŋta, Mallard duck (64)
Pakŝiŋ, Kidney (81)
Paŋpaŋna, Soft (37)
Pasu, Nose (80)
Pe´tiżaŋżaŋ, Lamp (27)
Peżi wacipi, Grass Dance (90)
Peżihu´tasapa, Coffee (53)
Peżu´tasapa, Coffee (53)
Pi, Liver (81)
Pidamaya, Thank you, I am proud of you (13)
Piye, S/He/It fixes/repairs (something) (34)
Po´ġe, Nostrils (80)
Psiŋ, Rice (53)
Pŝin, Onion (53)
Pte, Cow, cow buffalo (62)
Pte People, Servants to the spirits (42)
Pte´cedaŋ, Short (36)
Pute, Upper lip (80)
Putehiŋ, Mustache (80)

Þo, Fog or mist (9)

Ġa, and (27)

Sanksaŋ nica, Dress (82)
Saŋ'pa, More (16)

Sa´pa, Black (16)

Siceca, Child (11)

Sicoǧaŋ, Calf (body part) (81)

Sicu, Sole (81)

Siha, Foot (81)

Siŋteŝda, Rat (63)

Siŋtomni, Dakota value, cycles (60)

Sioux, An Ojibwe word meaning "snake" (3)

Sipa, Toes (81)

Sipahuŋka, Big toes (81)

Sisitoŋwaŋ, People of the Fish Village (4)

Siyete, Heel (81)

Ska, White (16)

Som, More (contraction) (16)

Su, Wheat, seed, or grain (48)

Suŋ´ka, Younger brother (78)

Suta, Hard (37)

Ŝa, Red (16)

Ŝa, S/He/It shouts or yells (21)

Ŝahdoǧaŋ, Eight (15)

Ŝake, Nails (81)

Ŝakowiŋ, Seven (15)

Ŝa´kpe, Six (15)

Ŝa´pe, Dirty (37)

Ŝa´pesni, Clean (37)

Ŝazi, Orange (16)

Ŝdo´ŝdodaŋ, Meadowlark (64)

Ŝi´ca, Bad (37)

Ŝiĉe, Brother-in-law (Female usage) (79)

Ŝina uŋpi ŝkehaŋ wacipi, Fancy Shawl Dance (90)

Ŝiŝoka, Robin (64)

Ŝiyo, Pheasant (64)

Ŝkaŋ, S/He/It moves about (21)

Ŝkata, S/He/It plays (21)

Ŝni, Negative: not, no (28)

Ŝukciŋcadaŋ, Colt (63)

Ŝuŋciŋca, Young wolf (63)

Ŝuŋgmanitu, Wolf (63)

Ŝuŋǧbdoka, Stallion (63)

Ŝuŋǧidaŋ, Fox (63)

Ŝuŋǧina, Gray fox (63)

Ŝuŋǧwaŋiyaŋpi, Dog or horse, domestic (63)

Ŝuŋĥ'panda, Puppy or little dog (62)

Ŝuŋĥpanna, Puppy or little dog (62)

Ŝuŋ´ka, Dog, a generic term for dog-like animals (27)

Ŝuŋkatokeca, Wolf (63)

Ŝuŋ'kawakaŋ, Horse, common (27)

Ŝuŋkonaŝoda, Pacing horse (63)

Ŝuŋtaŋka, Horse, alternative (27)

Ŝupe, Intestines (81)

Ta, Moose (62)

Ta, Ruminating animals (generic) (62)

Ta taŋkaha, Buffalo leather (82)

Tabdo´ka, Bull buffalo or male deer (62)

Taciŋca, Fawn (62)

Tado´, Meat (53)

Taha, Leather (82)

Tahaŋ´ŝi, Male cousin (Male usage) (78)

Taĥaŋ, Brother-in-law (Male usage) (78)

Ta´ĥca, Deer (abbreviated) (27)

Ta'hcanowaŋpi, Sheep, domestic (62)

Ta'hcanskaŋa, Sheep (62)

Ta´hiŋca, Deer (27)

Tahiŋ´casaŋ, Antelope (62)

Tahu, Neck (80)

Takoża, Grandchild (78)

Taku, What (52)

Ta´ku econ, Busy (37)

Ta´kuna ŝni, Nothing (16)

Tamaheca, Skinny (36)

Tanaǧidaŋ, Hummingbird (64)

Taŋcaŋ, Body (80)

Taŋcaŋ akan, Upon the body (81)

Taŋcaŋ mahed, Inside the body (81)

Taŋ´ka, Large (37)

Taŋ-ka´, Older sister (Male usage) (78)

Taŋke´, Younger sister (Female usage) (78)

Taŋ´kŝi, Younger sister (Male usage) (78)

Taŋ'yan, Sell/good (37)

Tapuŋ, Cheek (80)

Tasŋaheca, Striped squirrel (62)

Taspaŋ, Apple (53)

Tataŋka, Buffalo (62)

Tate´, Male spirit, the Wind (40)

Tatokaŋa, Goat (62)

Tatuyetopa, Tate's Four Sons (43)

Tawinye, Cow buffalo, cow elk, or doe deer (62)

Tažuŝka, Ant (65)

Te´ca, New (36)

Tezi, Belly or stomach (81)

Ti, S/He/It lives (somewhere) (20)

Tibdo, Older brother (Female usage) (78)

Tiohnake, The immediate household (73)

Tioŝpaye, Dakota extended kinships (39)

Ti´pi, Dwelling (27)

Ti´tonwan, Dwellers on the Plains (4)

Tiwahe, The immediate family (73)

Tka, But (27)

To, Blue (16)

Tohan, When (52)

Tokahe, The First One (43)

To´keca, Dakota value, Changes (60)

To'keca, Why (52)

To'kiya, Where (52)

Tokŝu, S/He/It transports (something) (34)

Tokŝu´, S/He/It transports (65)

To´nana, Few (16)

To´pa, Four (15)

Tostan, Purple (16)

Tuĥmaġa han´ŝka, Wasp (65)

Tuĥmaġa, Bee (65)

Tu´kiha, Spoon (54)

Tukte, Which (52)

Tunkan, Father-in-law (Male usage) (78)

Tunkan'ŝi, Father-in-law (Female usage) (79)

Tunkan'ŝi, Paternal grandfather (11)

Tunkan'ŝi, Paternal grandfather (Male usage) (77)

Tunŝka, Nephew: sister's son (Male usage) (78)

Tunwin, Aunt: father's sister (78)

Tunžan, Niece: sister's daughter (Male usage) (78)

Tuwe, Who (52)

Tužan, Nephew: brother's son (Female usage) (79)

Tužan, Niece: brother's daughter (Female usage) (79)

U, S/He/It comes (48)

Uka, Skin (81)

Unzeoġi, Pants or trousers (82)

Un, S/He/It is, uses, or wears (48)

Unci, Maternal grandmother (11)

Unci, Maternal grandmother (Male usage) (77)

Unci, Mother-in-law (Female usage) (79)

Unciŝicedan, Crow (aka the bad grandmother) (64)

Un´kan, Maternal grandfather (11)

Unkcekiĥa, Magpie (64)

Unkitawa, Ours (51)

Unkiye, You and I (51)

Unkiyepi, We (51)

Unktomi, Spider (65)

Unŝika, Poor or pitiful (37)

Upan, Elk (common) (62)

Waboga un'pi ŝke'han wacipi, Men's Fancy Dance (90)

Waci´, S/He/It dances (34)

Wacinhnuni, Absent-minded (37)

Wacipi, Powwow, "They dance" (90)

Waditake, Brave (37)

Wahanpi, Soup (27)

Wa´hnawotapi, Table (27)

Waĥpanica, Poor (without money) (37)

Waĥpe baksaksa yutapi, Salad (53)

Waĥpekute, Shooters Among the Leaves People (3)

Waĥpetonwan, People Dwelling Among the Leaves (3)

Waĥu´pa koza, The fowl family (64)

Waihakta, Affectionate (36)

Wakan, Sacred (60)

Wakan wiconi, Dakota value, Sacred life (60)

Wakanheža, Child, sacred one (77)

Wakan´ka, Wife to Wazi (42)

Wakantanka, Great Spirit or The Creator (4)

Wak´ŝica, Plate (54)

Wakuwa, Hobbies (85)

Wambdi, Eagle (alternative spelling) (64)

Wamnaheza, Corn (53)

Wanaþin, Necklace (82)

Wanica, None (16)

Wan´ca, One (15)

Wanmdi, Eagle, or generic term for eagles (64)

Wanmdi, Royal or war eagle (64)

Wanmdi hdeŝka, Spotted eagle (64)

Wanmdi zi, Golden eagle (64)

Wanmdiduta, Red eagle (64)

Waŋ´ske, Fourth-born daughter (11)

Waŋya´ke/a, S/He/It Sees or perceives (65)

Wapaha, Cap (82)

Wapaha wapoŝtan, Hat (82)

Wa´pi, Lucky (37)

Waŝte, Good (37)

Waŝteda, Cute (37)

Waŝtedake, S/He/It likes (something) (86)

Waŝtewadake, I like (something) (53)

Wa´ta, Boat (27)

Wati, I live (13)

Watoto, Green (16)

Watuka, Tired (37)

Wawicaḳupi, Dakota value, True learning (60)

Wazi, Ruler of the Pte People who is later banished (42)

Wažuŝteca, Strawberry (53)

We, Blood (81)

Wi, The Sun (40)

Wica, Man (abbreviated) (11)

Wicada, S/He/It believes (something or someone) (45)

Wicahca, Elder male, 45+ (75)

Wicaĥcana wacipi, Men's Traditional Dance (90)

Wi´cape, Fork (54)

Wicaŝta, Adult male, 20–45 (75)

Wicaŝta, Man (11)

Wicauŋpi, Man's shirt (82)

Wiciŋcaŋa, Girl, 3–10 years old (74)

Wiciŋyaŋna, Girl (11)

Wico owotaŋna, Dakota value (60)

Wicohaŋ oŋ wo´wicakupi, Giveaway (given away to the crowd) (90)

Wicohaŋ wakaŋ topa, Dakota value (60)

Wiconi, Life (60)

Wihake, Fifth-born daughter (11)

Wikcemna, Ten (15)

Wikcemna napciŋwaŋka, Ninety (15)

Wikcemna noŋpa, Twenty (15)

Wikcemna noŋpa som ŝakpe, Twenty-six (16)

Wikcemna ŝahdoġaŋ, Eighty (15)

Wikcemna ŝakowiŋ, Seventy (15)

Wikcemna ŝakpe, Sixty (15)

Wikcemna zaptaŋ som zaptaŋ, Sixty-one (16)

Wikcemna topa, Forty (15)

Wikcemna yamni, Thirty (15)

Wikcemna zaptaŋ, Fifty (15)

Wikoŝke, Girl, 6–11 years old (74)

Wikoŝke, Young woman, 11–20 years old (74)

Winona, First-born daughter (11)

Wiŋ, Woman (abbreviated) (11)

Wiŋuhca, Elder female, 45+ (75)

Wiŋuŋpi, Woman's shirt (82)

Wiŋ´yaŋ, Woman (11)

Wiŋ´yaŋ, Adult woman, 20-45 (75)

Wiŋ´yaŋ ahana wacipi, Women's Traditional Dance (90)

Wi´pi, Full of food (37)

Wi´tka, Egg (48)

Witko, Foolish (37)

Witkosŋi, Sober (90)

Witkotka, Crazy (37)

Wi´yatke, Cup (54)

Wi´ži'ca, Wealthy (37)

Wo´ahope Oco´wasiŋ, All Observation (59)

Wo´caŋtewaŝte Ocowasiŋ, All Benevolence (59)

Wo´caŋtohnakapi Ocowasiŋ, All Generosity (59)

Wo´hdaka, S/He/It chats, converses, talks (34)

Wo´iyokihi Ocowasiŋ, All Values (59)

Wo´kicaŋpte Ocowasiŋ, All Consolation (59)

Wo´ksape, Wisdom (59)

Wo´ksape Ocowasiŋ, All Wisdom (59)

Wo´ksape topa, Dakota value, Four wisdoms (60)

Wo´ohoda Ocowasiŋ, All Respect (59)

Wo´okaĥniġe Ocowasiŋ, All Knowledge (59)

Wo´okihi, Dakota value (60)

Wo´okiye Ocowasiŋ, All Peace (59)

Wo´onspe, Lesson (19)

Wo´ope, Female spirit, brings pleasure and harmony to a home (40)

Wo´owotaŋna Ocowasiŋ, All Honesty (59)

Wo´petuŋ, S/He/It shops (45)

Wo'ŝicaoŋa, Dakota value (60)

Wo´takuye Ocowasiŋ, All Relatives (59)

Wo´te, S/He/It eats (54)

Wo´tehda, S/He/It is hungry (45)

Wo´wa, Purity (76)

Wo´waciŋtaŋka Ocowasiŋ, All Patience (59)

Wo´waditake Ocowasiŋ, All Bravery (59)

Wo´wakaŋ, Lifeline of innocence or sacredness (76)

Wo´wakinihaŋ Ocowasiŋ, All Courtesy (59)

Wo´wanaġoptan Ocowasiŋ, All Obedience (59)

Wo´waonŝida Ocowasiŋ, All Kindness (59)

Wo´wapi, Book, letter, paper (27)

Wo´wapiska, Paper (white) (27)

Wo´waŝtedake Ocowasiŋ, All Love (59)

Wo´waŝteohŋa, Dakota value (60)

Wo´wicada Ocowasiŋ, All Trust (59)

Wo´wicake Ocowasiŋ, All Truth (59)

Wo´wicowaĥba Ocowasiŋ, All Humility (59)

Wo´wiĥa, Funny (37)

Wo´wiyuŝkiŋ Ocowasiŋ, All Joy (59)

Wo´yuonihaŋ Ocowasiŋ, All Honor (59)

Wo´yute, Food (27)

Wo´żu, S/He/It plants, sows (34)

Wo´żuha, Empty bag or sack (48)

Wo´żuhadaŋ, Small bag (48)

Ya´mni, Three (15)

Yuhe/a’, S/He/It has or possesses (52)

Yu´te, S/He/It eats (something) (54)

Zani Waŝte, Good health (13)

Za´ptaŋ, Five (15)

Zi, Yellow (16)

Zica´, Squirrel (63)

Zi´ġi, Orange (16)

Zitka´, Bird, also generic term for all bird-like creatures (63)

Zitka´mdeġa, Pelican (63)

Zitkahdeŝka, Spotted bird (63)

Zitkaŋa, Bird (36)

Zitkaŋasapa, Blackbird (63)

Zitkaŋaŝa, Red bird (63)

Zitkaŋato, Bluebird or blue jay (63)

Zitkataŋka, Big bird (63)

Zito, Green (16)

Zizica, Turkey (64)

Zuzuhecedaŋ, Snake (64)

The text of *Beginning Dakota / Tokaheya Dakota Iapi Kin* has been set in Minion Pro. Inspired by classical, old-style typefaces of the late Renaissance, this Adobe Original typeface was designed by Robert Slimbach. The first version of Minion was released in 1990, Cyrillic additions were made in 1992, and finally the OpenType Pro version was released in 2000.

Book design and composition by Wendy Holdman.
Manufactured by Sheridan Books, Ann Arbor, Michigan.